5/12

JUN 2 1976

artifacts of Prehistoric America

artifacts of Prehistoric America

Louis A. Brennan

Photographs and Illustrations by Harold Simmons

Stackpole Books

ARTIFACTS OF PREHISTORIC AMERICA

Published by
STACKPOLE BOOKS
Cameron and Kelker Streets
Harrisburg, Pa. 17105

Printed in the U.S.A.

Library of Congress Cataloging in Publication Data

Brennan, Louis A

    Artifacts of prehistoric America.

    Includes index.

    1. Indians of North America—Antiquities. 2. Indians of North America—
Implements. 3. North America—Antiquities. I. Title.

E77.9.B72   732'.2   75-20386

ISBN 0-8117-0174-3

Contents

Foreword

THE OBJECTIVE OF this *ana* on artifacts and technologies of Stone Age America is modest and specific. ("Ana: a collection of miscellaneous information on a particular subject." The American College Dictionary.) It is to assemble within the covers of a single volume of manageable size the verbal and visual descriptions of the customary tools, equipment and material possessions of the Amerind—the American aborigine—and enough information about their manufacture, presumed use and cultural placement to make them comprehensible as archaeological data. Thus the bias of the book, in its principles of selection and arrangement and in its intended usefulness, is toward the archaeologist-prehistorian.

What appears herein is the result of personal experience, which is not to be confused with caprice. It is what the author—who has spent almost three decades in archaeological excavation, in reading, in attending conferences, in informal debate and discussion, in writing books and papers, in lecturing and, above all, in editing archaeological journals—believes the beginner (either as academic or independent student) should learn as quickly as possible. This is not the whole vocabulary of American archaeology, but it is a glossary of the principal nouns, with a sprinkling of the active verbs, without a knowledge of which the language would be perplexing if not unintelligible. It was not the author's intention to compile an encyclopedia or dictionary or any kind of comprehensive reference; it was his intention to provide such definitions, explanations and visualizations as would facilitate the absorption of archaeological literature at one level and the identification of archaeological objects at another.

Archaeology is a rapidly growing and changing body of knowledge. What is consensus explanation today, or fact (as of current knowledge), or accepted conclusion based on known evidence can be altered or reversed at any time by last season's excavation. Any book on archaeology, American or Old World, is at the mercy of the latest discovery, be it in the field (a very recent dig in Pennsylvania has produced the earliest date for man east of the Mississippi; it is 15,000 C-14 years) or in the hard sciences on which archaeology depends (that the calendar year age of events in the millenia B.C. are variably older than their C-14 year ages), and this book can claim no exemption. There are, doubtless, statements in it that will become obsolete within the next few years. But it does not seek to teach archaeology; concerned with definition and description and the basic concrete, it seeks only to prepare for archaeology to be learned, as quickly and as pleasantly and as profitably as possible.

L.B.

Acknowledgments

I OWE THANKS to the following for unrepayable favors in conducting me and my collaborator, Harold Simmons, through their collections and permitting unrestricted photography:

Herbert Kraft, professor at Seton Hall University and Director of the Seton Hall Center for Archaeological Research, for access to the collections of the Center and to his own incomparable private collections.

Charles Gillette, Curator for Archaeology, New York State Museum, for access to the Museum's collections and personal assistance in the selection of items for photography.

David Thomas, Curator for North American Archaeology, American Museum of Natural History, for throwing open the cased collections of the Museum while the North American collections were in process of renovation and re-housing.

Ronald Thomas, State Archaeologist of Delaware, for access to the collections of the Island Fields Museum and for personal attention to our photographic needs.

Richard Regensburg, of the Delaware's Division of Archaeology staff, for demonstration of his custom-built atlatl.

Much material from the Briarcliff College Museum and Laboratory for Archaeology and the author's personal collections was also used.

L.A.B.

chapter 1

About Artifacts And Their Classification

THE OLDEST DIRECTLY dated artifact, that is, article of human manufacture and for use, known in the present record of American prehistory is a bone "flesher," made from the tibia of a caribou and found at Old Crow, Yukon Territory, Canada, in 1966. Since bone is organic or once-living material it can be dated by the C-14 (carbon 14 or radioactive carbon) method of age assay. Submitted for laboratory processing by C-14 assay, the flesher yielded an age of 27,000 plus 3000 or minus 2000 C-14 years. This expression of the result of the laboratory test means that the probable age of the flesher, a toothed tool for scraping away the fascia or inside membrane of an animal hide, lies between 25,000 (27,000 minus 2000) and 30,000 (27,000 plus 3000) C-14 years.

Care must be taken in reporting ages obtained by C-14 test since C-14 years are not necessarily equivalent in duration to solar, that is, calendar years. It has been demonstrated by comparing ages obtained by C-14 assay with absolutely dated tree ring ages from the long-lived bristlecone pine—specimens 7000 years old have been located in the White Mountains of California—that at about 2200 years ago there begins to be a widening discrepancy between solar and C-14 years. The C-14 year becomes increasingly longer as a trend, so that at about 6000 C-14 years ago the real or solar-year age would be about 6700 years. How the discrepancy veers after 6000 C-14 years ago has not yet been determined; it may continue the widening curve or it may turn downward again toward equivalence with solar time, or less. At the order of the age of the flesher there is now no way of calculating, by comparative dating, the correlation between C-14 and solar age. But the margins of error set forth in the laboratory result of assay of the flesher—which are, by the way, margins of statistical probability, not laboratory uncertainty—are sufficient to make allowance for all likely discrepancy.

A table for converting C-14 dates into solar years back to about 7000 years ago has been published in *Archaeology of Eastern North America, Vol. 2, No. 1,* Bronson Museum, Attleboro, Massachusetts.

The flesher was found in a deposit of river gravel, not at a habitation site with other tools or cultural evidence of the people who made it, though it was associated with some other bone that had been obviously cut with a sharp-edged tool. Singular, and without cultural association, the flesher tells us little about the culture of the time (*culture* is an umbrella word covering all the specifics of human activity, from fire-making to city building, from stone industry to shamanism) except that a rather "sophisticated" bone tool for hide working had been made with the use of another tool, presumably of stone. To begin at the beginning—if not in time, in primitiveness of culture in America—we must fly southerly some 5000 miles to Ayacucho Valley, Peru, opening on the Pacific Ocean.

AYACUCHO

During the late 1960s a team of scientists headed by Richard S. MacNeish, one of America's leading archaeologists and the archaeological discoverer of the American origin of maize, made a thorough survey of the prehistory of Ayacucho Valley, which heads up high in the Andes mountains. One of the sites dug and analyzed was Pikimachay, or Flea Cave, about 9000 feet above sea level where, at the very bottom of the cave fill, 20 feet deep in places, were found the extremely crude stone tools used presumably by the Valley's earliest settlers.

Four stone artifacts were recovered from this bottom stratum, of the rudimentary chopper-flake tradition of stone industry, the same technological level at which stone toolmaking began among the incipiently human Australopithicines of East Africa about 2 million years ago. This is not to say that the Pikimachay tools are of anything like the same age; the chopper-flake tradition, as it happens, met the tool needs of early man so well that even though the stone workers of Africa and Europe had developed well beyond it by 500,000 years ago, it persisted in Eastern Asia, from whence came the earliest Americans, until perhaps 20,000 years ago. It continued as an element in almost all American stone industries until the 20th century.

The "chopper" is a large flake of stone, or a split pebble minimally chipped at one end to a cutting edge and used for chopping, hacking, heavy scraping, shaving (of wood), sawing, and digging. The flakes of the tradition are smaller chips removed from a pebble or parent block of stone which have, on removal, ready-made sharp edges suitable for cutting and scraping, and much the same tasks as on a smaller scale chopper. Until the invention of steel the edges of chips of such stones as flint, obsidian, quartz, and quartzite were, though brittle, the sharpest tool edges available to man. From the first moment that he deliberately chipped a stone for the resulting sharp edges of flake and parent block or core, man possessed the secret of all tools up to the age of screws, nuts, and bolts. Hammers and drills excepted, no matter what the tool, it is the sharp edge that does the work.

The lowest stratum of chopper-flake tools at Pikimachay also contained, fortunately, some bone of an extinct variety of sloth. The laboratory result of dating this material was a C-14 age of 19,600 plus or minus 3000 years, which could mean on the plus side (the more probable side) a C-14 age of 22,600 years. It falls, therefore, in MacNeish's view, within a general cultural "horizon" or time level with similar assemblages of stone tools from Heuyatlaco, Mexico (C-14 date 21,800 years), from Tlapacoya, Mexico (C-14 date 23,150 years), and from Lewisville, Texas (C-14 date 38,000 years), with all dates having been obtained from associated bone, shell or charcoal.

Whether the earliest habitation of America was 100,000 years ago, as MacNeish suggests, or 40,000 years ago, or 25,000 years ago, as the foregoing ages suggest, it was certainly as early as 20,000 years ago at Pikimachay, for the cave had its sloth-hunting occupants for the next 12,000 years, on the evidence, some of which is C-14 dated. That evidence shows an evolving stone industry technologically derived from the chopper-flake tradition. Elsewhere in Ayacucho Valley the evidence covers the time from about 8000 years ago to A.D. 1500, the time of the Spanish conquest, from the level of hunting and gathering to farming and village communities. Ayacucho Valley affords a record of 20,000 years of human habitation.

With 20,000 years accepted as a date at which much of the scant population of America was at a minimum level of cultural and technological development, it should be clear what an undertaking it is to compile a digest and dictionary of American Stone-Age artifacts. By about 3000 years ago Amerind culture had developed in stone work alone from the simple fracturing of pebbles and blocks of stone to the monumental sculptured heads of La Venta, Mexico. And not only did culture elaborate during the intervening years, it diversified as local populations adapted tools and strategies to exploit the thousands of specific local environments of the North-South American land mass, stretching from the North Pole almost to the Antarctic Circle. A book such as this cannot hope to cover exhaustively such an illimitable amount of material. Its intent must be restricted to mainstream developments, to satisfy the student's need to know rather than the savant-specialist's intensity of interest.

TIME SEQUENCE

The scope will be the Stone Age of the New World up to the "high cultures" or civilizations of Mexico and Middle and South America. The focus will be on the Stone Age of America north of Mexico, the cultural remains of which are most likely to be found or seen in collections by those most likely to consult this reference. In chronological terms this scope is:

25,000 B.P. (B.P.—before present) to 14,000 B.P.—the unspecialized lithic or pre-stone projectile-point period.

14,000 B.P to 12,000 B.P.—the Early Hunter period

12,000 B.P. to 8000 B.P.—the Paleo herd-hunter period

11,000 B.P. to

4500 B.P. in the Southeast

3000 B.P. in the Northeast
2000 B.P. in the Southwest
A.D. 1500 on the Pacific Coast
A.D. 1800 in the Northwest
—the Archaic hunter-gatherer period
From the end of the Archaic to the time of contact with Europeans—the Ceramic period

None of the foregoing bracket dates are to be taken as absolute boundaries. Stone projectile points may have been used as early as 16,000 B.P. The Archaic pattern of hunting and gathering in environments outside the habitat territories of large herding animals such as the mammoth may be and probably is older than the Paleo herd-hunter pattern. The beginning of the manufacture of ceramic pottery has a widely uneven chronology. But some kind of time scheme must be used and the above appears to be the least subject to major revisions. It will be detailed later in the chapter on projectile points.

The artifacts with which this book will deal can only be those that survived weathering and other agents of disintegration. Since the stones commonly used during the Stone Age—the flint family, quartz, quartzite, argillite, slate and shale, rhyolite, basalt and sandstone are to all intents and purposes imperishable, it is not too much to say that every stone artifact ever made or its fragments, and all the debitage of cores and waste flakes are still in existence, in the earth or in collections. At the same time 99 percent of the artifacts surviving from the Stone Age are stone. Still, a surprising number of artifacts, probably broadly representative of types used, of organic materials—wood, bone, antler, horn, hide, hair, and plant fiber—have been preserved under fortuitous circumstances. Deposit in dry caves in semi-desert regions, burial under volcanic ash or lava flows, sealing off by flood deposits of chemically inert clays and sands, discard in heaps of acid-neutralizing shell, continuous immersion in water—all these have provided preservative matrices. Without such chance natural embalming, much of Stone-Age archaeology would be conjecture.

MATERIAL

The material of which they are made provides the primary determinant in the classification of artifacts, crossing categories of form and function, because the material determines the technology. The major inventory divisions in which archaeologists report their finds and the classification used herein are as follows:

Stone
Chipped stone: tools, ornaments
Polished (ground or rubbed) stone: tools, ornaments, pipes
Rough stone: tools, altered pebble "images"
Organic: animal
Bone, antler, shell: tools, ornaments, utensils
Organic: vegetal
Plant fibers: basketry, textiles
Metal: tools, ornaments

Ceramics
Pottery utensils, ceramic ornaments, pipes

As an attribute the body material of an artifact is an important clue and direction of study. In the case of stone, whether the parent material is pebble or quarried affects technology and size of artifacts; the location of the source geographically can tell much about population movement and trade relations; a preference for high quality material over more available low quality material has cultural implications. But body material is only a secondary attribute in identification.

Many types of artifacts were made in two or more materials. Projectile points (spear heads, arrow points, dart points, harpoon heads) were made of stone, bone, antler, wood and metal; cooking vessels were made of stone as well as of fired clay, and of water-tight basketry in the stone-boiling method of cookery; beads were made of anything that could be perforated for stringing, including snail shells and seeds; pipes were made of baked clay, stone and, if the shaman "sucking tubes"—the probable predecessors of the pipe—are counted as pipes, of bone.

TOOLS AS BEHAVIOR

Nor is formalized shape quite the definitive attribute, at least not without the wear evidence that shows why the type is what it is. The objective of archaeological-anthropological research is human behavior under a specified set of conditions, its consistency, its adaptability and the cause and meaning of change, for human behavior follows, as animal behavior does not, a line of options intelligently and pragmatically chosen. Artifacts are precise—so precise as to be often half-enigmatic—statements of behavior, declarations of intention achieved in order to achieve further intentions in the experience of living. Archaeology discovers artifacts within the context of their deposit; anthropology attempts to interpret them as personal and social behavior.

To achieve an archaeological-anthropological digest, then, it is necessary to provide some such information as this:

1. Present the artifact itself by illustration (which is the equivalent of discovering it in the ground).
2. By name or short description identify its use or presumed use.
3. Point out its important attributes of form and use.
4. Suggest its known cultural and time placement and distribution.

But when these simple and obvious obligations are applied to the construction of a classification by material and artifact types anomalies appear that throw a linear cataloguing out of balance, anomalies that are caused by the relative commonness or rarity of types, by the complexity of their technology and by their significance as diagnostics of culture phases, traditions or horizons. Chipped stone technology is far more complex than that of grinding-abrading; stone projectile points are not only the most diagnostic stone artifacts, they are more variable in form than any other, and that diagnostic variability covers 10,000 years, at least, of American Stone-Age prehistory. Even after the introduction of ceramic pottery, when it became a primary diagnostic and time marker, projectile points retain, for the most part, their diagnostic value since the manufacture of ceramic pottery was a trait adopted by diverse groups who already had their own projectile point traditions. As to ceramics, no less variable and diagnostic within an horizon, the recoveries from intensely occupied sites are so bewildering in their overwhelming thousands of sherds that so many "types" can be created out of the scores of variables that "typing" approaches the subjective.

chapter 2

The Technology of Chipped Stone

THE FIRST STONE artifact ever created was a flake of stone knocked off a pebble by a blow from another pebble. That chip became an artifact when the man (or proto-man) who had struck it off used its naturally sharp edge to cut, saw or scrape meat, wood, bone or hide. When that user, having worn the sharpness off the edge of the flake, struck a second flake off the pebble or parent core, he had invented an industry. When he struck off a third flake and noticed that he was, while producing flake tools, effecting an edge on the core as a by-product, and he used that core to chop or dig or gouge, he had invented the rudiments of the lithic technology by which men were to live for the next 2 million years.

Perhaps manlike beings had used lengths of wood or bone or antler as clubs or levers or pokers or stabbers, and these were the first implements; but until they had the cutting edges to shape implements to their purposes, they were not toolmakers. The first humanoid to strike off a flake-knife-scraper was Adam and all those he taught to strike off tool-flakes were his progeny, the genealogy of man.

PERCUSSION

Nothing would seem to be simpler than the act of bringing down a stone held in one hand against a stone held in the other with a simple, direct movement of the arm. As an act stone percussion is indeed simple, but the elements involved are not. The flake may be removed from either the striking, that is, the moving stone, or from the target or stuck stone. And the hammer need not be a stone at all; it may be a club or baton of wood, bone or antler. And how is the stone held? In the hand, so that it gives appreciably with the blow struck against it? Or on the knee or soft earth, so that it gives somewhat less? Or on a hard rock? If it rests directly on the rock, the under rock serves as an anvil; but if it is held slightly above the anvil rock, there are two percussions or blows on the target stone. All of these are factors in the size and success of the flaking technique.

Nine rough bifaces or blanks. They may have been abandoned because they were not working down thin enough. This is the stage that all biface tools had to pass through. All were worked down from pebbles.*

LOCUS OF THE BLOW

And what about the site or locus of the blow? When the angle of the strike is wrong neither the striking nor the struck stone will release a flake; one or both will show only a little pit of pulverization. Blows struck at the right locus, at the correct angle, and with a force calculated to the resistance, can detach a large or small flake, a round flake or a parallel-sided, knife-blade-like flake, or they can sheer a pebble or a block in half.

An artisan-Adam could not have known all the things he was doing right when he struck off that first artifactual chip. Only the experience of doing them puzzlingly wrong as

* In this and all subsequent illustrations the long bar of the scale denotes one inch, the short bar one centimeter.

well as accidentally right could have instructed him in that pristine world in the rules and regulations of stone fracture, and they are many. His first lesson would be that he had to have an angled edge or lip (in stone tool technology this is called a striking platform) as the locus of his strike and that he had to concentrate the force of the blow there with a small hammer face. The force of the blow on stones that fracture conchoidally (most of the hard stones) diffuses from the point of impact down through the core mass in a cone. (The premise here is that the stone is of uniform structure, not faulted nor shot through with impurities nor unevenly crystalline). The flaking blow must be struck at a locus on the lip at an angle that will cause the perimeter of the cone of force to travel downward parallel to the face of the core. Depending on the angle and how near to the edge of the striking platform that the blow falls the flake will be razor-thin, or thick and therefore useful as a secondary core, if it is not wanted itself as a tool. The good flintsmith has to know what he wants and how to get it.

TECHNOLOGICAL TERMS

One would think that some of the first words in the human vocabulary had to be technological terms related to flint working. There must have been a monosyllable, at least an inflected grunt, for the all-important striking platform; it had to be recognized and isolated by the eye in flaking control and it remains on the end of the struck flake where the flint worker had, in some tools, to get rid of it. Integral with the striking platform is what modern students call the "bulb of percussion," a swelling in the stone at the locus of impact rather as though the

On the left are struck flakes. Nos. 1, 2 and 3 show broad striking platforms grouped toward center. These flakes show the dorsal or outside surface. Nos. 4, 5 and 6 show the ventral or core side. Small scar at the bulb of percussion on No. 4 is called the bulbar scar or erailleure. A stem was chipped into No. 6; it is an end scraper.

striker's blow had raised a bruise there. The "positive" bulb of percussion, the swelled manifestation of the bulb, is to be found on the flake; the "negative" or concave manifestation is to be found in the core, often accompanied by a "bulbar scar" or "erailleure." The bulb of percussion is the center of visible concentric ripples in the inner surface of the flake (the ventral side) which are the palpable evidence of how the force of the striker's blow travels down through the core mass. Because these ripples occur, somewhat like the ridges in a clam shell, and the normal flake has somewhat the same shape, the stones that are affected this way by chipping are said to break conchoidally, that is, like a shell.

(The innate disposition of flints and similar stones to fracture conchoidally can be overcome but the techniques for doing this, to produce *flake blades,* long flakes with parallel sides, like table knife blades, was not employed extensively until about 40,000 years ago. The beginning of flake blade making is coincident with the appearance of Homo sapiens, modern man, who either invented it or first realized the potential of blades as an advance in toolmaking. The cardinal principles in flake blade making is in the preparation of the striking platform and the calculation of the angle and force of the strike.)

PLATFORM CREATION

The first flintsmiths must have sought out pebbles or blocks of stones with natural lips or edges for striking. But there must have occurred to them, early on, that they would have to prepare their own striking platforms, especially where the supply of raw materials was in river pebble form, since rounded river pebbles usually present only an egglike exterior. As it happens, however, pebbles can be split in two at almost any point with a single blow. The trick is to lay it lengthwise on an anvil, which may even be the thigh, leaving part of it projecting over the anvil unsupported. A quick rap, with follow-through, at a point on the unsupported length sheers the pebble in two at the point of impact, leaving the two parts each with a simple striking platform circumference. It was easy, then, to pare down the core

A prepared core and flake blades. Note negative bulb of percussion at top of core. No. 2 has been fitted with a stem for hafting. No. 4 shows curvature of flake blades struck from prepared cores; the curvature usually increases as blades are struck nearer the center of the core.

Three cores from which flake blades have been struck

by striking off flakes all around. The good flintsmith planned his work so that he shaped the tool or tool preform that he wanted while he was thinning down the core.

Much has been made up to now of the importance of a lip or striking area against which to deliver an effective blow. But what if the worker found that where he needed to strike off a flake to proceed with his work he had only a sharp edge to strike against? It must be pointed out that when there are no more edges to strike against the worker is finished, whether the tool is or not; rejected cores that cannot be flaked any more litter the sites of flintsmiths. But for probably 12,000 years or more the Amerind flintsmith has had a simple strategy for dealing with this impediment of the sharp edge. Using an abrading stone—of sandstone or granite or the like—he dulled the sharp edge until it was thick enough for a striking platform, and then used a soft hammer baton to strike off the flake. The flake thus struck will probably show no bulb of percussion and is called a "resolved" flake. The trick works, however, only under the right circumstances which include a skilled hand on the hammer.

TWO TRADITIONS

The fact is that the artisan-Adam who struck off the first artifactual flake invented not only lithic industry, but two traditions within that industry, the flake tradition and the core tradition, which can also be designated respectively the uniface and the biface tradition. Since the flake is an instant tool and since flakes can be struck off in a wide range of sizes and thicknesses to suit the task at hand, depending on the size of the core material, the flake tradition is the first born to the two. In a pure "flake industry" the core was simply a block of flake-yielding stone from which flakes were struck off until it would yield no more, after which it was discarded or put to rude use, as for pounding. If any additional work was to be done to shape up the flake, it was done on the dorsal, or outside face, and on the sides. The ventral or inside face of detachment from the core was left untouched, hence flake industries are uniface industries. The flake blade industry of Homo sapiens just mentioned was a

uniface industry, as was the non-flake blade industry of Neanderthal Man, called the Mousterian.

A core industry produces bifacial tools. It is a process of chipping away at the core material, as in sculpting or whittling, until that core is reduced to the wanted shape, with flake obverse and reverse faces. The chips are struck off as need be for the shaping of the core, without regard for shape or future utility. They become mere debris ("debitage," to the archaeologist), like a pile of whittler's shavings. This does not prevent them from being used as casual or pickup tools, nor from being retouched into tools when they have the right attributes. The term "core industry" equals "bifacial industry," though flakes can also be converted into bifaces, since they are also cores.

AMBIVALENCE IN AMERICA

Evidence is increasing toward certainty (with discoveries like Pikimachay) that the first immigrants from Asia, before 25,000 years ago, brought with them a chopper (incipient biface) and flake (uniface) industry and American lithic industry retaining, in the main, this ambivalent character throughout its history. It did not follow the classic lines of exclusively uniface or exclusively biface lines of development known in Europe and Africa. Nearly all Amerinds made stylized projectile points and knives, scrapers, celts and axes (when these were not made by grinding), choppers, drills, chisels, etc. in bifacial forms. Stone projectile points, in particular, are almost exclusively bifacial all over the Western Hemisphere. But this bifacial backbone of American lithic industry did not preclude the pickup use of billions of flakes as knives and scrapers, or their quick fashioning, by a strike or two, into perforating or graving or reaming tips, or scrapers or concave scrapers or "spokeshaves," or the retouch of any of these to restore or even off an edge.

Yet no one who has ever dug or collected from a site of lithic industry in America will doubt for a moment, from the evidence of cores, rejects, blanks or preforms (the preform is the intermediate form between the core and the finished tool) of bifacial tools and fragments thereof, that the preoccupation was with bifacial tools, from whatever material—pebble, quarried stone and flakes.

There were two centers of uniface flake blade industry in Stone-Age America, one in Alaska and one in Mexico. The Alaskan center resulted from a later immigration of hunters from Asia in what, in Old World terms, would be called a Late Paleolithic stage of industrial development; that is, they practiced a variant of the flake blademaking tradition of Homo sapiens. This immigration may have been as early as 15,000 years ago or as late as 10,000 years ago, and is not to be confused with the immigration of the chopper-flake people of Pikimachay. Blademaking technology spread from Alaska southward along the Pacific Coast but it is not likely that this spread was responsible for the flake blademaking technology that developed in Mexico; the lapse in time and the hiatus in geography is too great, and there is no known cultural link between the Northwest Coast and Mexico.

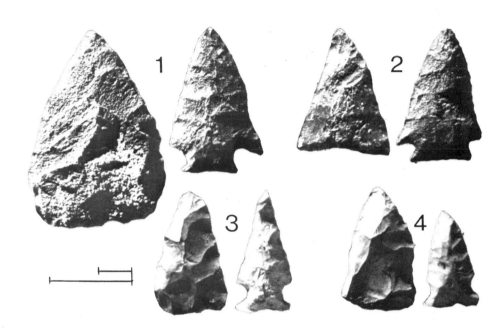

Four preforms and the kind of projectile points made from them. The preforms have been reduced to the necessary thinness and are ready for final shaping.

The Mexican flake blademakers are responsible, however, for the two flake blademaking traditions north of the border, the Poverty Point (a Louisiana place name) culture of the Lower Mississippi, at about 4200 years ago, and the Hopewell of Ohio and Illinois of about 2000 years ago. But both of these cultures turned out conventional biface projectile points—knives, ceremonial blades, preforms and cache blades. (Cache blades are preforms stored for later finishing into tools.)

TREATMENT OF STONE

The storage of preforms brings up the matter of the treatment of stone, particularly flint and chert (which is what the geologist calls impure flint) to make it or keep it workable. The caching of preforms and less formally worked supplies of material was almost always in moist ground to prevent, it is thought, the stone's turning brittle through loss of what is called the "water of constitution." Since cache blades are blanks or preforms worked at the quarry or source of material, such as a pebble beach, they are covered with flake scars which accelerate the drying-out process by exposing more surface. Over the short term drying makes flint brittle; over the long term it creates a tough cortex or rind that is more refractory to flake than the interior stuff.

If damp storage was the treatment for stored materials, the treatment immediately preceding work seems to have been the exact contrary; it was, the evidence from broad areas seems to show, a heating of the material. Don Dragoo of the Carnegie Museum found at the Wells Creek Crater site in Tennessee certain evidence of preheating of core material as early as 12,000 years ago, and perhaps earlier. There are two evidences of preheating, discoloration of the material and "pot-lid" fracturing. A pot-lid fracture is a dishlike flake scar in the body of the core, usually where no strike could have caused it; pot-lid fracturing can easily be proved by experiment. The most obvious discoloration of stone by heat occurs in yellow jasper, a color phase of flint. Quarried brown or yellow jasper will turn, on exposure to heat, to one of several shades of red. The discoloration is usually only a skin-deep patina. But many kinds of flint will discolor, usually to red, when heated.

Because direct exposure to fire causes the undesirable pot-lidding, the assumption is that core materials about to be worked were heated in hot water or by some other indirect method. Modern experimenters agree that heat treatment does improve the workability of flints, cherts and other cryptocrystalline stones, though it is not necessary to fine workmanship. Not all pot-lid fractures, of course, are evidence of heat treatment; many of them were simply accidental, as debitage or cores came in contact with hearths in the routine of living.

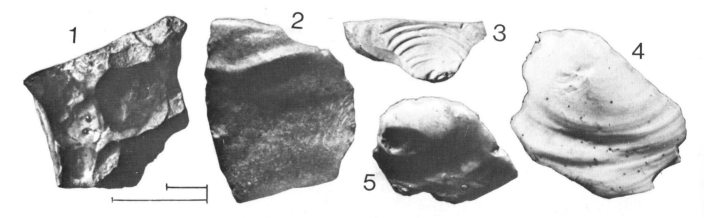

No. 1 shows heat-produced pot-lid flake fracture. Nos. 2, 4 and 5 are typical conchoidal flakes. Nos. 3 and 5 show conchoidal ridges or ripples. Bulbar scars are visible on No. 4 and No. 5 at bulb of percussion.

CHIPPING TECHNIQUES

Direct percussion of stone, with the target stone held in the hand or resting on the knees, on the ground or against another stone is the unavoidable first technique in stone working; it would be impossible to say which holding was first, since all will work and all "come naturally," so all may be regarded as having existed from the beginning. This produces, as we know, a bulb of percussion at the point of the strike. There is another technique which produces two bulbs of percussion, one at either end of the flake. If the target stone is held an inch or so above an anvil stone, and is driven into the anvil stone by the worker's blow, both ends of the core receive impact simultaneously and cones of force drive into the core from each end. No attempt will be made to explain why the resulting flake, with two bulbs of percussion, was found desirable, but the technique appears to have been used only in the chopper-flake stage. The excavator or collector who comes upon a series of such flakes should treasure them as evidence of something that merits intensive investigation.

There is, incidentally, another aberration of flaking, the "hinge" flake. When the force of the chipper's blow does not travel entirely through the core, the flake will break off somewhere in mid-core; its terminus will be a snubbed, rounded end rather than the sharp, thin edge that occurs when the flake runs the length of the core. The effect is easy to identify by the bluntness where the flake "hinges" out of the core. The hinge flake can only be the result of a mis-stroke. There is very little likelihood that a hinge flake was ever intentional, since it may well have ruined the core.

To the many variables in the holding of the target stone must be added the use of clamps and lodgements, though these were probably more often used in indirect rather than direct percussion, as will shortly be explained. And to the many variables in the posture of the target stone must be added the variables in the striking stone. Weight and balance were of first importance, as was the presence of some kind of bulge or projection or slant that made possible a strike with a small hammer face. Also, the hammer stone used in flintsmithing had to be as hard or nearly as hard as the material being chipped.

The hammerstone, No. 7, was all that was needed for a 17-year-old self-taught flint-smith to produce Nos. 1 - 6. The horsehead, No. 6, was created by the young artisan to show his versatility with a hammerstone. Nos. 1, 2, 3 and 4 were made on pebbles.

When the aboriginal flintsmith had learned all this lore (and a great deal we don't know about besides), he could do very nearly anything he wanted to by percussion, even to fine retouch flaking. But there is one job direct percussion cannot do well, the working of narrow indentations and tight corners. Such work has to be done by indirect percussion or by pressure-flaking.

Indirect percussion is done by striking a punch held against the core with a hammerstone. Since the punch, of wood or antler, has a pointed but blunt end, it can be directed at any angle so as to make notches in cores or preforms. With the punch held in one hand and the hammerstone in the other, the target stone needs to be steadied in a clamp of some sort, or in a third hand. The hundreds of thousands of notched-blade projectile points made in America almost had to have been notched by indirect percussion or by pressure-flaking.

Cores and hammerstones. No. 1 and 3 are cores. No. 2 is an exhausted core used as a hammerstone. No. 4 is a very heavily used pebble hammerstone.

PRESSURE-FLAKING

In pressure-flaking a punch or "drift" is used but it is not struck with a hammerstone. The flintsmith merely presses the blunt point against the material he is working and twists. The flake detached is not from the pressure point but on the opposite, that is, the underside of the material. The flakes are tiny conchoidal ones. Anthropologist Richard Gould, in *Yiwara*, an account of a sojourn among the natives of Australia in the 1960s, reports that he has seen them pressure-flake with their teeth. Pressure-flaking is the quickest and simplest method of flaking and an utter tyro can learn it in a few minutes if he has good material to work with. It is the method favored by fakers of artifacts, by hobbyists and by those who make stone artifacts frankly for profit. But what the pressure-flaker needs is as good quality material as he can find. Bottle glass is excellent and obsidian, which is natural glass, is equally good; however, it must be thin, for the pressure exertable will not penetrate thick pieces. The pressure-flaker works on the edges almost exclusively. The modern hobbyist who works in flint usually obtains his material by hunting over aboriginal sites for suitable flake debitage; he can turn out a very fancy shape, using a suitable flake, in ten minutes or less.

Another stone-working technique employs a combination of indirect percussion and pressure-flaking; it is called punching. It was used in the production of flake blades where fine material was available as in the Valley of Mexico with its abundance of obsidian. The punch, in this method, is a long rod of wood with a blunt point on the distal or far end, and a crutchlike crosspiece at the proximal end. The workman, holding a properly prepared core on the ground with his foot or a clamp, placed the punch point on a lip of the core and leaned his chest forward into the crutch. His weight, conveyed to the punch point, was enough to literally push off a flake blade.

Many flakes which are descriptively flake blades (no very good name for this artifact has been found, though "strip blade" seems the most apt) can be found on stone industrial sites in America, but they are not flake blades in intention at all; they are simply a normally recurrent kind of chip. The diagnostic for the presence of a flake blade industry is the prepared core with a faceted striking platform. Flake blades can be recognized by the ridge running lengthwise on the dorsal side of the flake. This ridge is the edge of a prior flake scar, and the workman strikes directly above it to detach the blade. The first blades struck off a prepared core will be straight, but they become increasingly curved as they are peeled off closer to the center, the curve being inward at the bottom. The core becomes exhausted at the bottom rather than at the top or striking platform end, and ends up looking like half an egg. The excavator or collector who finds himself on a flake blade site should count himself lucky; he will find some very unusual tools and he must be alert to recognize them all, for many of them will be diminutive "microblade" tools of fascinating delicacy.

ARTIFACTUALNESS

It should not be presumed that the foregoing remarks on stone technology represent an in-depth presentation of the subject. It is the barest outline introduced with the intention of acquainting the reader with the most commonly used terms and of giving him some idea of what he is looking at when he sees a piece of chipped stone. In the widest sense, every piece of humanly chipped stone is an artifact. The degrees of "artifactualness" may be set forth thus, from least to most:

1. Debitage: the industrial debris of flakes that are the off-products of flint knapping.

2. Rejects: cores abandoned in work because the material was poor, because they broke or because the chipping plan was not going well.

3. Utilized flakes and cores that have been used without further work.

4. Flakes or rejects that had been minimally touched up to enhance an inherently useful feature.

5. Fragments of artifacts used after breakage.

6. Blanks or preforms: these are the stages through which a biface passes between the original hunk of parent material and the finished artifact, but they are often tools in their own right, as wear patterns will show. They should always be examined closely for signs of

use. Without those signs of use they still are high in "artifactualness" because they are nearly realized tools.

7. Finished tools: in the sense of completed rather than refined, whether biface or uniface.

The student, as he gains experience, may find himself as interested in the first six degrees as in the final one. Considering their numbers he may be forced to be, as the complete botanist knows his weeds as well as his cultivated plants.

chapter 3

Stone Projectile Points

THE WEAPONS OR killing tools for which chipped stone points were made by Amerinds were the javelin or cast spear, the hand-held thrusting spear or lance, the harpoon or tethered spear, the dart or projectile shaft cast by the atlatl or throwing stick, and the arrow shot from a bow. The bow and arrow was the last of the weapons of chase and warfare to be adopted (or, less likely, invented) by Amerinds, its first use conventionally placed at about A.D. 1 in the Southwest and at A.D. 1000 in the Northeast.

The bow never did displace the atlatl and dart in some regions, however; the atlatl, an Aztecan word, continued as the army weapon of the Aztecs until the Spanish conquest and among the sea-hunters of the Arctic until this century. Of consideration to the latter, a bowstring is adversely affected by the humidity of sea air, and a bow is a two-hand weapon, while the atlatl leaves one hand free to maneuver the kayak.

Nor did the bow displace the spear or lance, especially among the equestrian Indians of the Plains where it was used in close combat and as a javelin on occasion. Non-equestrian Indians used it to kill buffalo by thrusting it into them as they grazed or charged, a supremely dangerous way to make a living but probably no more so than bullfighting.

The spear-javelin (it is technically a lance when carried by a horseman) was not man's first cast weapon. Probably it derived from missile clubs and stones (The late L.S.B. Leakey, discoverer of the earliest men in East Africa, has suggested that the bola was the first formal cast weapon.) A wooden shaft with a fire-hardened point that may be 250,000 years old was dredged up some decades ago from Clacton-on-Sea, England, and it would be no surprise if such an implement were as old as the manufacture of chips for knives; what would the knives have been used for if not to cut and scrape wood shafts?

In America such self-pointed shafts may well have been the weapon of the chopper-flake people of Pikimachay. Nothing in the tool kit of the lowest levels could have done in the sloths whose bones were found with them; a thrusting stick or spear at least would seem to have been a *sine qua non* for inflicting fatal wounds on this slow but menacingly-clawed prey. Finds from a stratum below Clovis, New Mexico of stone projectile points (12,000-11,000 years ago) suggest that points of bone may have been the first attached type of weapon head. Bone and antler or horn do well enough in piercing small or thin-skinned game and out of simple, bodkinlike points of bone there probably developed the harpoon head, a barbed point which hooks inextricably into the flesh of the target animal; it is made fast to the end of a line, the hunter retaining the other end, using it to play the game like a fish.

For penetrating efficiency, wood, bone, antler and horn projectile tips are easily surpassed by stone points, the best of which are not inferior to steel. Until their invention hunters were hard put to pierce lethally the tough pelts of big game animals like buffalo, mastodon and mammoth. The earliest stone projectile point in the Pikimachay sequence appears at about 11,000 years ago. But it is unifacial, and not in the tradition that produced the bifacial points that constitute overwhelmingly the mass of American stone points. The bifacial

Richard Regensburg of the Division of Archaeology, State of Delaware, shows the proper holding position for a spear cast from an atlatl. The atlatl and spear are of his own manufacture. The spear, or dart, is of sweet gum grown in pine woods shadow and cut during the winter when the sap is out of the shoot. It will be noted that the bannerstone is at the distal end, adjacent to the hook, rather than just behind the hand where many experimenters think it should be placed. In the Regensburg model the weight is a wood block, but it has been carefully sized to about 4 oz., about the weight used by Mau (see text), who placed the weight near the hand.

tradition seems to have sprung up in South America and to be represented by bifaces from Venezuela that may be as early as 14,000 years ago. Bifacial, stemmed points of about 13,000 years ago from Oregon seem to be the earliest stone projectile points of any kind found within the present boundaries of the United States. By 11,000 years ago, bifacial chipped stone projectile points were being used all over the Western Hemisphere, even to land's end in South America.

Although it appears that the dart is about to be catapulted, the proper throwing motion is to keep the dart and atlatl in contact on a straight, horizontal line throughout the entire casting action; the atlatl adds to the length of time of this contact, in effect lengthening the arm. The dart being used is composite, with a long back shaft and a short foreshaft, about half the length of an arrow shaft. The back shaft falls away when the dart hits its mark. The short fore-shaft allows the projectile point to be used as a knife.

BALLISTICS

The ballistics of the shafted, stone-tipped projectile have not been as thoroughly tested as they might be. What has been established is that there has to be a balance between the weight of the shaft and the point somewhat forward of the midpoint so that the shaft will not skew nor tumble in flight. Each projectile had to be individually made and balanced. Long heavy shafts require heavy points; light reed shafts can carry only lighter heads. But it is not easy to determine by the size of a point just what kind of weapon it was used on.

Tests have shown that large points, up to about 2 inches long, can be used on arrows. But the larger the point the higher the trajectory at which it must be shot, so that unfletched (unfeathered) arrows are not very practical missiles. But a fletched arrow cannot use a large point; the "balance" of the fletched arrow is achieved by the air resistance of the feathering. The rule of thumb that a stone point less than 1.75 inches long may be an arrow point is not a bad one. On the other hand it is not a reliable one, either. Many types of small points archaeologically too old to have been arrow points turn up on sites all over the New World. Some of these are simply points used on light reed shafts; others are undoubtedly evidence of the use of the composite dart.

The composite dart consists of two parts, a foreshaft and a backshaft. The foreshaft, of the dimensions of an arrow, carries the stone point. Its distal end fits into a dowel hole in the forward end of the back shaft, the rear end of which is also dowelled to fit the hook of the atlatl. When the projectile is cast the foreshaft penetrates the target and lodges there, while the back shaft falls away, to be retrieved and used again. The advantages of the composite shaft are not well understood, but such shafts have been found in contexts as old as 6000 years.

The throwing motion at mid-cast. The atlatl has been shown to add 58 to 60 percent to the distance attained by a hand-thrown spear. The projectile shaft is also much more controllable.

Release point. Regensburg has discovered that the dart travels better and does not lose distance when cast into the wind, a matter of great importance to the hunter approaching the quarry from downwind.

SHAPE

As important as the size-weight correlation is in the analysis of stone projectile points, the attribute used by archaeologists to identify them culturally is shape. Because they have such variability of shape and because they are the most numerous of stylistically variable artifacts (of which there are few in American chipped stone industries), projectile points are often the only "fingerprint" identification available to the archaeologist in sorting out a cultural sequence.

Looked at as a tool, the projectile point consists of two parts: the blade or acting part, and the shank (haft or tang) which connects the working part to the "handle," the shaft. Many kinds of projectile points are shankless; they consist of the blade only, which is slipped into or attached by one means or another to the end of the shaft. They can be classified in simple geometric plane forms. But most projectile points are shanked, the shank being either a stem or an opposition of notches in the blade. These factors permit a plane form taxonomy: as follows on pages 34-36.

CLASS A   SHANKLESS

Pattern I Arcuate (bow-sided)

Style 1 Lanceolate   **Style 2 Ovate**

Types

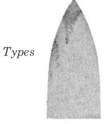         

Flat base   *Concave base*   *Round base*   *Pointed base*

Style 3 Trianguloid

Types

Pattern II Rectilinear (straight edged)

Style 4 Triangular   **Style 5 Pentagonal**

Types

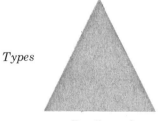      

Equilateral   *Isosceles or*   *Flat base*   *Concave base*
                      spirate

CLASS B   SHANKED

Pattern III Stemmed

**Style 6
Semi-stemmed**   **Style 7 Full stemmed**

Types

| | *Square* | *Contracting* | *Flare* | *Pinched* | *Shoulderless* |

Subtypes comprise several variations on the length and breadth of the stem in relation to the blade and treatment of the base of the blade.

Pattern IV Notched Blade

Style 8 Side-notched (the axis of the notching of the blade is perpendicular to the altitude, thus -1-)   **Style 9 Corner or bias notched blade (The axis of the notching is at an acute angle from the corner toward the altitude /1   )**

Types

Base as wide or wider than shoulders   *Base narrower than shoulders*   *Notching at corner*   *Notching above corner*

Style 10 Basal notched (the notching is from the base)

Types

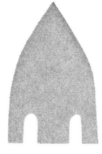 

Double notched   *Single notched or bifurcate*

Style 11 Neck-and-Yoke (A combination of stemmed or notched shank and basal concavity produces projections called, despite the anatomical inappropriateness, "ears.")

Types

Notched   *Stemmed*

The foregoing is a taxonomy of outline plans of projectile points only, not what archaeologists call a typology, which is a catalogue of the forms in which the three-dimensional, ponderable, well or ill made specimens actually occur. The late Daniel Josselyn has calculated that 2592 variations are possible within this taxonomy. All American projectile points will fall into one or another of the shapes in the taxonomy but this is far from saying that points that fall into the same style or type, as the word is used above, are in any way related.

What the archaeologist calls a "type" is a collection of points of the same description which can be shown to be culturally related, with the similarity in description being one sign of the relationship. This kind of typology is not systematic, not taxonomic. There seems to be no way it can be systematized.

Some "types" are horizon styles; that is, they are found over wide regions within a time stratum of perhaps a millenium or more. The Clovis Fluted Lanceolate is such a horizon style, found from the Arizona-Mexican border to Nova Scotia, in the millenium between 11,500 and 10,500. The Kirk point is also a horizon style for at least 500 years throughout the southeastern United States, and into Michigan in the Midwest and New York in the Northeast. On the other hand it is sometimes a feature that is the horizon marker, as in the bifurcate point, in which a basal notch has split the point base into two legs. This feature appears on many types of points not otherwise related, at about 7500 to 6500 years ago. In other instances such as the small, stemmed Lamoka point of the Finger Lakes region of New York, the type name has been used loosely for a whole technological family of points.

To say that the typing of projectile points is not taxonomic is only to say that no way has been found, or at least generally adopted, for arranging kinds of points into horizon styles, wide area types, areal subtypes and local varieties that is culturally valid. Three great traditions run through the entire history of projectile point manufacture, the shankless, the stemmed and the notched blade, but the changes rung in these forms as they evolved are not according to any discoverable principle. In making his differentiations the typologist has to deal with a long list of attributes, primary, secondary and random, knowing that all of them have a meaning, in technology, in hunting practice or in some other aspect of culture. Some attributes and features which have type-determinant value are:

Size range: The size-weight correlation as a ballistics factor has already been discussed. Most types of points, however, occur in two, three, or even four modes of size, from miniatures to mega-points. The range may be explained, using the ballistics argument, by assuming that several kinds of material were available for shafts and/or that a range of shaft lengths was used for hunting different kinds of game or for hunting under different conditions, i.e. forest, meadow, shoreline or scrub growth. Very large points may often be explained as being knives or daggers, since all they needed to be used as knives or daggers was a short handle instead of a projectile shaft. The tip of a projectile point is useful as a perforator, reamer, drill or punch, and the blade edges are useful as knives, saws or scrapers. None of these uses destroy the point's utility as a weapon head. When a projectile point form is recovered in a wide range of sizes it may well be that it is a generalized tool form and projectile points were only one of the tools made in that form.

Proportions: A slight change in proportions makes great change in the "look" of a point and, very often, in its type. The number of valid "types" that can be recognized by specialists must now number close to 500. (Nobody can identify all of them, of course.) These types are all variations in proportion of the relatively few patterns and styles listed in the shape taxonomy. Among the stemmed points there are wide blades with wide stems, wide blades with narrow stems, wide blades with long stems and innumerable combinations of width and length proportions as well as treatment of bases and shoulders. In the notched points the depth and placement of the notches and the shaping of the base below the notches are variables that have to be taken into careful account in typing.

Chipping: Points of the same type will show the same chipping technique and the same sequence of flake removal. Some points are made by hard hammer alone, some by hard and soft hammer, some by these plus indirect percussion (in notching) and some with all these plus pressure-flaking for edge retouch. One of the most unmistakable chipping patterns is the rare "ripple" flaking in which tiny bladelike flakes are removed in parallel from the blade edge across the face of the blade, creating a striking corrugation of "ripple" effect. There are two kinds of ripple flaking; in the first the flake scars run from each edge to a median ridge; in the second they run from edge to edge across the face. Both are the ultimate in chipping artisanship.

Quality of workmanship: Many types of points, especially those of the simple stemmed pattern, do not require fine workmanship and ordinarily do not exhibit it. Other types can be achieved only by precision work. In still other generalized patterns, such as the triangles, the quality of workmanship distinguishes one type (or subtype) from another.

Material: Point types are often distinguished by the material of which the points are made. The Clovis Fluted Lanceolate makers and their immediate descendants would go long distances to obtain fine chert or flint. But for the so-called Lackawaxen points of the Delaware Valley at about 5000 to 4000 years ago the preferred materials were shale and argillite, with better materials such as flint, quartzite and quartz absent almost entirely. Most of the Archaic cultures used whatever materials were available from the immediate locality, neither importing stone nor travelling out of their territory for it. The quality of that material and its effect on the firmness of execution of design and sometimes created local varieties or subtypes.

Features: Several details of final form have determinant value.

Edge grinding: Most of the early hunter lanceolate and near lanceolate points are edge-dulled by abrasive grinding part way up the blade apparently to prevent fraying of the lashings by which the point was bound to the shaft. Triangle points are never edge-ground and stemmed and notched points do not need to be.

Basal and notch grinding: Most Early to Middle Archaic points were ground at the base for reasons that are not clear, and ground in the notches for the same reason the lanceolates were edge-ground, to prevent fraying the lashings. Notched points can usually be placed as early or late simply by the presence of basal and/or notch grinding. Early triangles (circa 5000 years ago) are often ground around the rim of the base, but this may be a base-thinning measure.

Basal thinning: Because they are inserted into the split end of a shaft most points are thinned by chipping and/or grinding to make for a less bulky closure of the split in binding the point to the shaft. But there is a lengthy series of stemmed points (but by no means all stemmed points) in which the stem remains thick and the base untreated. It is assumed that these stems were inserted dowel-like into the ends of reed or hollowed-out shafts and bound, or secured with gum or resin.

Bevelling: Two kinds of bevelling of the edges of projectile point blades have been noted. One, done by multiple retouch chipping, seems to be merely a chipping pattern or practice. It was once thought that this kind of bevelling of opposite sides and faces would cause the point to revolve in flight, like a rifle bullet. Simple experiment instantly proved this notion to be nonsense. Assuming bevelling was done for a purpose (and was not a manufacturing technique), that purpose may have been to provide a thickness just behind the edge so that the edge could be resharpened again and again. The second kind of bevelling is effected by removing a single long flake along the edge the full length of the blade. Its intent is decidedly to resharpen the edge and it is an artisan's trick, not a type-determinant feature.

Serration: Certain series of points in the Early Archaic of the Southeast and late horizons in the Southwest were edge-serrated or saw-toothed. The serration may be either coarse or fine, the two grades having, probably, different tool use purposes. The coarse grade was produced by indirect percussion and the fine, apparently by pressure flaking. Serration may be indicative of a class of tools rather than a type or sub-type of point, and may occur in any horizon.

Shoulder spurs: Projectile points, usually Archaic, will be observed which have more or less prominent extrusions at the shoulders. In some instances these have been left behind by the repeated sharpening of the blade above. What the usefulness of these spurs might have been nobody has deduced, though it is clear that they must have been considered useful or they would have been removed. Though the spurs are found only on certain types of points, they are not a type characteristics. But there are other types where a delicate spur has been worked into the shoulders. These are not barbs as such, and again may be indicators of a tool type, not of a type of weapon point. Nevertheless, the care with which they were made convinces that they had cultural significance.

Surely enough has been said by this time to make the point that projectile points are not mere souvenirs or knickknacks, but solid paragraphs of information about how their makers lived in a world in which they were the superior animals, but not all that dominant. To know that an artifact is a projectile point is a very low order of knowledge; to recognize its shape by the shape taxonomy, is a beginning of learning; to be able to identify types and know their significance is not yet expertise but it is as fundamental, even to the pride of ownership, as is knowing the countries of the world, and the continents on which they are located, to geography.

With an estimated 500 projectile point types having already been described, and more being added weekly, the typology to follow can present only the most noted variations on the three main themes. It is very likely that archaeologists will continue to segregate "types" which are actually subtypes or local varieties for years to come, but it is now almost certain in this second generation of recognition of the critical importance of "types" that all the plane outline variants possible within the three main traditions have been discovered and type-named.

Before a "typology" of projectile points is presented an exposition of the regional time scheme and chronological-cultural terms to be used is in order. The scheme, somewhat simplified, in most general use, for the United States is that in the accompanying chart.

The Chopper-Flake, Pebble Tool Horizon is that period which began at a time not yet certainly determined, but surely before 25,000 years ago, during which no recognizable stone projectile points were made. The tools range from crude choppers and flakes to increasing formalization of tool types based on bifaces and/or flakes.

The Early Hunter Period is that rather indefinite span of time, perhaps 1500 years, after the beginning of the manufacture of recognizable stone projectile points, when points were made in generalized lanceolate or ovoid biface forms. These points were used to bring down small as well as large game, but single quarry large game was definitely the object of the hunt.

The diagnostic of the Paleo-hunter period is the fluted lanceolate or ovoid point. The practice of "fluting" lanceolate or ovoid bifaces by driving out a channel or flute flake from the base longitudinally up the face spread by population expansion or by imitation throughout the entire middle of North America, from California to Nova Scotia, from Alberta, Canada to Florida. The people who used fluted points were hunters of herd animals, though this does not mean they subsisted only on a diet of mammoth, buffalo, horse or camel. The Paleo-hunters were once thought to have originated on the Great Plains, but it has become increasingly clear that they were much more numerous in what is now the Eastern Woodlands, not suitable environment for herd animals. However, before about 10,000 years ago, the prairies affording grassland grazing for herd animals extended across the southern United States into Florida and across the northern tier of states to the Atlantic. In this northern sector, south of the last stand of the Wisconsin glacier, herd animals would have been caribou and, possibly, the moose-elk, in addition to the mammoth. While the Paleo-hunter kill sites so far discovered show that the Paleo-hunters slew solitary animals at water holes or in bogs, the discovery at the Olsen-Chubbock site in Colorado of the bones of about 190 individuals of an extinct variety of bison with projectile points and other cultural material in an arroyo, dated at 10,150 years ago, demonstrated that the "drive" technique of herd hunting has long been in use where the environment favored herd animals. A way of

Archaeological Culture Chronology Chart

YEARS BEFORE PRESENT	EAST	MISSISSIPPI VALLEY	PLAINS	GREAT BASIN	SOUTHWEST	PACIFIC COAST
40,000	CHOPPER-FLAKE, PEBBLE TOOL HORIZON					
13,000	EARLY HUNTER					
12,000	PALEO HUNTER	PALEO HUNTER	PALEO HUNTER	EARLY HUNTER	EARLY HUNTER	EARLY HUNTER
11,000	EARLY ARCHAIC	EARLY ARCHAIC	PALEO HUNTER	EARLY HUNTER	EARLY HUNTER	EARLY HUNTER
10,000	EARLY ARCHAIC	EARLY ARCHAIC	PALEO TRADITION	DESERT CULTURE	DESERT CULTURE / EARLY HUNTER	EARLY HUNTER
9,000	EARLY ARCHAIC	EARLY ARCHAIC	PALEO TRADITION	DESERT CULTURE	DESERT CULTURE	EARLY HUNTER
8,000	MIDDLE ARCHAIC	MIDDLE ARCHAIC	PALEO TRADITION	DESERT CULTURE	DESERT CULTURE	EARLY HUNTER
7,000	MIDDLE ARCHAIC	MIDDLE ARCHAIC	PALEO TRADITION	DESERT CULTURE	COCHISE CULTURE	EARLY PERIOD
6,000	MIDDLE ARCHAIC	MIDDLE ARCHAIC	PLAINS HUNTER	DESERT CULTURE	COCHISE CULTURE	EARLY PERIOD
5,000	LATE ARCHAIC	LATE ARCHAIC	PLAINS HUNTER / PLAINS ARCHAIC	DESERT CULTURE	COCHISE CULTURE	MIDDLE PERIOD
4,000	LATE ARCHAIC	LATE ARCHAIC	PLAINS HUNTER / PLAINS ARCHAIC	DESERT CULTURE	COCHISE CULTURE	MIDDLE PERIOD
3,000	EARLY WOODLAND	EARLY WOODLAND	PLAINS ARCHAIC	DESERT CULTURE	COCHISE CULTURE	MIDDLE PERIOD
2,000 (A.D.1)	MIDDLE WOODLAND	MIDDLE WOODLAND	WOODLAND	SOUTHWESTERN TRADITION	SOUTHWESTERN TRADITION	LATE PERIOD
1,000 (A.D.950)	LATE WOODLAND	MISSISSIPPIAN	PLAINS VILLAGE TRADITION	SOUTHWESTERN TRADITION	SOUTHWESTERN TRADITION	LATE PERIOD
WHITE CONTACT TIMES c1,500						

life geared to single kill incidents when meat could be made by the ton has to be different in its pace and habits than one geared to smaller animals and plants as a subsistence base. Where there were herd animals to be hunted, as on the Plains, this herd hunting tradition never died out.

The Plano tradition was even more strongly a herd hunting economy, the only difference from the Paleo-hunter being in the projectile point forms employed. Plano periods points were mostly very well made lanceolates or lanceolates with incipient stems. This is the period of ripple flaking and high artisanship in lithic techniques.

The Archaic pattern of economy was a broad exploitation of all the food and material resources within a limited territory by hunting and foraging. It was a continuation, with stone projectile points, of the hunting-gathering life of the chopper-flake tradition. It is a living off the land, keyed to what the land produced in most abundance. Herd hunting is a specialization; the hunting-foraging pattern is the way most people lived throughout human history, with locally abundant food resources—fish, large herd animals or vegetal produce inducing specializations.

For the archaeologist the Archaic period ends with the adoption of ceramic pottery, called the Woodland period over the eastern two-thirds of the present United States. Actually it came to an end only with the introduction of plant cultivation or farming. The Woodland, however, means to the archaeologist all the time between the beginning of the use of ceramic pottery to the period of contact with Europeans. In the Southeast the ceramic period begins about 4500 years ago; in the Northeast about 3000 years ago; in the Midwest about 3000 years ago; in the Southwest about 2000 years ago; on the Pacific Coast there never was a ceramic period. Some form of plant cultivation began in the Eastern Woodlands outside the Northeast about 2000 years ago, and in the Northeast about A.D. 900; in the Southwest it began at about 4500 years ago, according to the evidence of very primitive forms of maize discovered in Bat Cave, Arizona. It is clear that plant cultivation and the manufacture of pottery bear no cultural relationship to each other. It was not until fields began to be cleared and planted that there was any real change in settlement pattern. Villages occupied most of the year, date from the beginning of agriculture. Only during the Late Woodland does there seem to have been any need to fortify these villages. But the arrival of influences from Mexico, associated with corn-beans-squash agriculture wrought considerable enrichment of the material culture beginning shortly before 2000 years ago and resulted in such cultural efflorescence as the Hopewell "Mound Builders", and later, the Mississippian temple mound builders. With the appearance of European trade goods on aboriginal sites, the American Stone Age comes to an end and the ethnographic, if not the historic, period dawns.

The following list of 80 projectile point types illustrates no more than about 20 percent of the types named and described in the voluminous literature. But the list does make reference to many of these types where there is a similarity in theme. The fact is that all the major themes in projectile point shape, with the exception of the double basal-notched, were present in point manufacture by no later than 10,000 years ago. They kept recurring, though not in straight line traditions, until the end of the use of stone projectile points.

Further comments about the projectile point types accompany the illustrations and are correspondingly numbered.

EARLY HUNTER

1. Sandia

Age: 12,500 to 11,000 B.P. (before present), estimated.

Range: The Southwest (Arizona and New Mexico) into Idaho and Canada. Sandia Cave, the type site, is near Albuquerque, New Mexico. Examples have been sporadically reported from east of the Mississippi.

Detail: 2″ to 4.5″ long. Base may be squared off or rounded. Some specimens are fluted, that is a long flute or channel flake has been removed from the base, running up the long axis of the point, as in the Clovis and Folsom fluted points.

Comment: The term "Sandia" applies to a specific culture limited to the Southwest. The theme of half-stem or single shoulder is more widespread. Compare with Milliken points of Canada and the Panamint Stemmed of desert California.

2. Lake Mohave

Age: 11,680 to 9940 C-14 years ago, dates from Nevada.

Range: desert Southwest, including California, to Canada through the Great Basin.

Detail: 2.5″ to 3.5″ long; broad percussion flaking.

Comment: The type site, Lake Mohave, is an extinct lake in now desert southern California. The lake was in existence when the Lake Mohave people lived on its shores.

3. Silver Lake

Age: Falls within the time span of Lake Mohave points.

Range: approximately that of Lake Mohave points.

Detail: 1″ to 1.75″ long; a distinctly short dart point.

Comment: Extinct Silver Lake is in the Mohave Desert of California. The Silver Lake may be a variation of the Lake Mohave point. It may not be as old by 500 years or so.

4. Cascade

Age: 10,500 to 8000 B.P., based on C-14 dates.

Range: From the Northwest (Washington and Oregon) southward through California into the desert Southwest.

Detail: 2″ to 5″ long.

Comment: The diagnostic point type for the Old Cordilleran complex of hunting-fishing-gathering peoples of the Northwest. The type name derives from the Cascade Mountains of the region. This bipointed theme is found all over the West and is probably also represented by the Lerma (see below).

5. Gypsum Cave

Age: 10,455 to 8527 C-14 years, by contextual evidence at the type site, Gypsum Cave, Nevada.

Range: New Mexico and Nevada.

Detail: 2″ to 2.5″ long.

Comment: Found with evidence of the hunting of now extinct sloth and camel. The Morrow Mountain point type of the Southeast is very similar in form and manufacturing attributes but dates about 1000 years later.

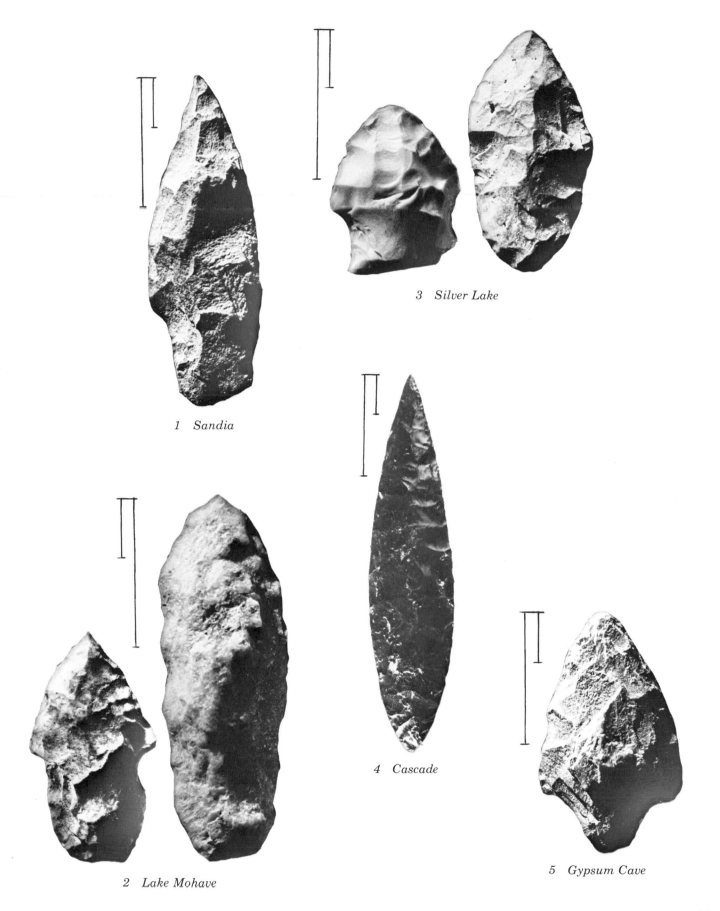

1 Sandia

3 Silver Lake

2 Lake Mohave

4 Cascade

5 Gypsum Cave

43

6. Lerma

Age: 10,000 to 7500 B.P., estimated.

Range: From mid-Mexico into Texas and across the Southeast as far as Georgia.

Detail: 2″ to 5″ long; thick in mid-blade and thinned at each end. Usually rather crudely made.

Comment: The Lerma, as such, is associated with the last of the big game hunters in the Mexican highlands and may be related to the El Jobo big game hunter points of Venezuela. But the willow leaf shape occurs widely in early horizons though not in as yet identified contexts.

7. Panamint Ovate

Age: 9000 to 7500 B.P., estimated.

Range: Desert California and southern Great Basin.

Detail: 2.5″ to 3.5″ long; broad percussion flaking.

Comment: Named for Panamint Dry Lake, in desert California. A diagnostic of the Panamint culture which frequented the shores of the lakes and bogs that once dotted the now arid Great Basin.

8. Pinto Basin

Age: 8000 to 6500 B.P., on geologic evidence.

Range: Arizona and desert California. The name derives from the Pinto Basin, an extinct lake in desert California.

Detail: 1″ to 1.75″ long; edges of blade sometimes serrated or sawtoothed. A thin, notably small point.

Comment: The Pinto Basin point is very like the LeCroy of the same time level found in the East, from Alabama to Michigan and, rarely, into southern New York.

9. Danger Cave W-41

Age: Two C-14 dates from Level II at Danger Cave, Nevada, where this type was found, are 9789 and 8960 B.P.

Range: Desert Culture of Great Basin; restricted in distribution to central Great Basin.

Detail: 1.25″ to 2″ long; percussion-flaked with some edge retouch.

Comment: This type marks the first recorded appearance of the simple triangle, without stemming or notching.

PALEO-HUNTER

10. Clovis

Age: 11,850 B.P. (average of two C-14 dates at the Lehner site in Arizona) to 9250 B.P.; C-14 date at the Naco site in Arizona.

Range: From the Rockies eastward to the Atlantic coast, with a few specimens from California sites. The south-north distribution is from Guatemala to Nova Scotia. The heaviest concentration appears to be in the Southeast—Alabama, Georgia and Florida. The type site is Clovis, New Mexico.

Detail: 1″ to 4.5″ long. The flutes are relatively short and may appear on one or both faces. The yoke base and the blade edges to about one-third of the length of the point are usually ground smooth. Several techniques were used to draw the flute flake.

Comment: Though some Sandia points are fluted, the Clovis is regarded as the father of the fluted point tradition. The makers were, in the West at least, hunters of the big game herding animals, particularly mammoth.

11. Folsom

Age: 10,700 (by C-14 date) to 9500 B.P., estimated.

Range: The type site is Folsom, New Mexico. The Folsom, as such, is regarded as a High Plains (New Mexico to Colorado) type but Folsomoid points are of about the same distribution as Clovis.

Detail: 1.25″ to 2.25″ long. Folsom differs from Clovis in that it is thinner, has a longer flute and out-flaring "ears" at the base. It is basally and edge-ground and flutes are usually on both faces.

Comment: Folsom points are found with the bones of extinct varieties of bison but not with mammoth, horse, or camel, presumably because these were extinct by Folsom times.

6   Lerma

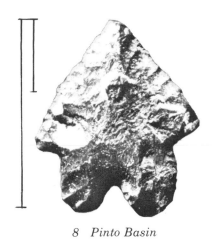

8   Pinto Basin

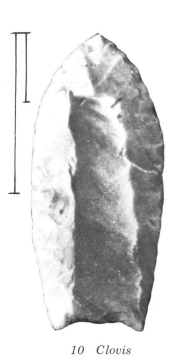

10   Clovis

9   Danger Cave W-41

7   Panamint Ovate

11   Folsom

12. Cumberland

Age: 10,500 to 10,000 B.P., estimated.

Range: Most of the territory east of the Mississippi, excluding New England. Named for the Cumberland region of Tennessee.

Detail: 2″ to 3.5″ long. The outline is Folsomlike but the type runs distinctly larger.

Comment: This may be an eastern refinement of Clovis, as Folsom is certainly a western refinement. The Beaver Lake type of Alabama to Florida, and the Suwanee and Simpson types of Florida and Georgia have similar outlines but are unfluted or weakly fluted and may be younger.

13. Quad

Age: 10,000 to 9500 B.P., estimated.

Range: The Southeast, from Alabama to the Ohio River. The Quad site is in Alabama.

Detail: 1.5″ to 2.5″ long. Proportions give it the appearance of a stubby Clovis. Weakly fluted. Edges usually ground.

Comment: Thought to be a variant of the Cumberland. Compare with the Golondrina of Arkansas-Oklahoma-Texas and the Holcombe, below.

14. Holcombe

Age: 10,500 to 9500 B.P., estimated from geologic context at the Holcombe Beach type site in Michigan.

Range: Upper Midwest and Ontario.

Detail: 1.5″ to 2.5″, usually less than 2″. Stubby in proportions. About half are fluted, on one face only.

Comment: Association is with Midwest caribou herd hunters.

15. Meserve

Age: 9000 to 8500, estimated.

Range: High Plains and prairies east to the Mississippi. The Meserve (personal name) site is in Nebraska.

Detail: 1.25″ to 2.5″ long; weakly fluted, with bevelled blade edges. Ground basal edges.

Comment: A non-lanceolate fluted point, thought to be transitional from fluted points. Comparatively rare but related to the much more abundant Dalton type of the Mississippi Valley and eastward to the Atlantic.

16. Hell Gap

Age: 10,850 (by C-14) to 9500 B.P., estimated.

Range: High Plains and southern Canada. The Hell Gap type site is in Wyoming. A very similar and probably related type is the Rio Grande of New Mexico and the Rio Grande valley.

Detail: 2.25″ to 3.5″ long. Basally and basal edge-ground.

Comment: Though sometimes found on sites with Folsom fluted points, the Hell Gap runs more to the Cascade and weakly-stemmed tradition of the Northwest.

17. Pentagonal (no type name)

Age: 10,000 to 8000 B.P., estimated.

Range: East of the Mississippi.

Detail: 1.5″ to 2.5″ long; ground base and basal edges.

Comment: An infrequent type found in late Paleo-hunter contexts. Can be confused with preforms for other types.

12 Cumberland

13 Quad

14 Holcombe

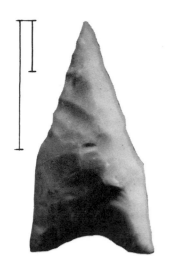

15 Meserve

16 Hell Gap

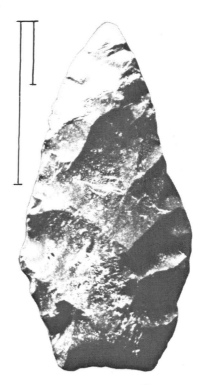

17 Pentagonal

PLANO HUNTER

18. Agate Basin

Age: 9500 to 9000 B.P., range of C-14 dates.

Range: From High Plains to Ohio, from Texas to Alaska, that is, throughout bison herd territory. Agate Basin is in Wyoming.

Detail: 2.5″ to 6″ long. Flaking is parallel collateral, that is, tiny, narrow flakes are removed in parallel from each blade edge, leaving a medial ridge the length of the blade.

Comment: The oldest of the parallel flaked points.

19. Plainview

Age: 9170 (by C-14) to 8000 B.P., estimated.

Range: From Northern Mexico to Alaska, from Wyoming to Louisiana. The type site is in Texas.

Detail: 2.5″ to 3.5″ long. Sometimes parallel-flaked, with basal and basal edge grinding. Parallel-edged rather than lanceolate in outline.

Comment: Of the same "family" as the Midland and the Milnesand types of the southern Plains. Like the Agate Basin, a bison hunter point.

20. Scottsbluff

Age: 9524 to 8826 B.P. by C-14 dates.

Range: High Plains and prairies, from Wyoming to Oklahoma and from Texas to mid-Canada. Scottsbluff is a Nebraska place name. Some few have been reported from east of the Mississippi.

Detail: 2.5″ to 6.5″ long. Collateral parallel-flaked, with basal and stem edge grinding.

Comment: The Eden type, of the northern Plains, an unstemmed lanceolate type, often with parallel flaking running from edge to edge across the blade, seems to be fraternal with the Scottsbluff. Also of this "family" are the Alberta of western Canada, the Holland of the Midwest, and the Frederick and San Jon of the southern Plains.

21. Allen

Age: 7900 (by C-14) to 7500 B.P., estimated.

Range: Northern Great Plains, with the Browns Valley type of Minnesota an eastern variant. The Allen (personal name) type site is in Montana.

Detail: 2″ to 6″ long. Oblique parallel flaking. Ground base and basal edges.

Comment: Has also been called the Yuma and the Colorado.

22. Angostura

Age: 8000 to 6000 B.P., estimated, though an Angosturalike and a Scottsblufflike point was found with a mammoth kill at Santa Isabel Iztapan in northern Mexico. The mammoth is presumed to have been extinct by 10,000 B.P. at the latest.

Range: The Great Plains, excluding the prairies, from Mexico to Canada. Angostura Basin is in Wyoming.

Detail: 2″ to 6″ long. Random (non-parallel) flaked. Occasional basal and basal edge grinding.

Comment: Originally called the Long (personal name) type from the Long site in South Dakota. May derive from the Hell Gap tradition.

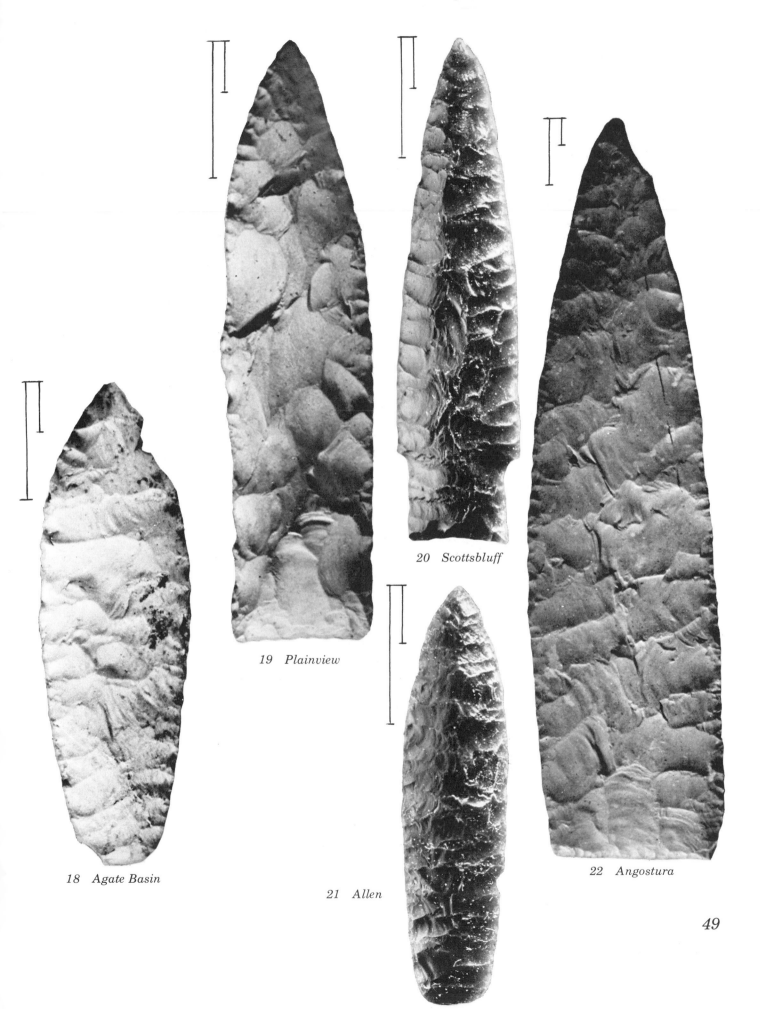

18 Agate Basin

19 Plainview

20 Scottsbluff

21 Allen

22 Angostura

49

ARCHAIC HUNTER-GATHERER

23. Dalton

Age: 9640 to 8920 B.P, by series of C-14 dates.

Range: From the Mississippi valley eastward south of the Ohio River. The Dalton type site is in Missouri.

Detail: 1.5″ to 3″ long. Usually weakly fluted and often edge-serrated or bevelled. Basally and basal edge ground. Blade often narrowed by resharpening.

Comment: The similar Meserve is regarded as final Paleo-hunter, the Dalton early Archaic, that is, the Meserve-makers were herd hunters, the Dalton-makers forest hunter-gatherers. Several varieties are recognized—the Colbert, the Greenbrier and the Hardaway-Dalton. Also called Breckenridge.

24. Big Sandy I

Age: 9500 to 6000 B.P., estimated from finds at the Dalton level of the Stanfield-Worley Rockshelter in Alabama and from sites in Tennessee.

Range: The Big Sandy is less a discrete type than a family of varieties on the same theme of broad, side-notched blade. This theme is found throughout the entire Eastern woodlands region. Big Sandy is a Tennessee place name.

Detail: 1.75″ to 2.75″ long. The base, basal edges and notches are ground. Usually basally-thinned, with a very short, flutelike flake scar in the middle.

Comment: The type has many local offshoots, such as the Brewerton side-notched of New York and the Godar of the lower Missouri River valley.

25. Raddatz

Age: 8000 to 7000 B.P., estimated from stratigraphy at the type site, the Raddatz Rockshelter in Wisconsin.

Range: Specifically the Upper Midwest, but the form and attributes appear all over the Midwest and elsewhere under other names, the Osceola of the Old Copper Culture of Wisconsin, the Hemphill of Illinois, the Graham Cave of Missouri, the Matanzas of the eastern prairies, Danger Cave W25 and W26, the Otter Creek of Vermont-New York and the Bolen Side-notched of Florida.

Detail: 2″ to 3.5″ long. Basal, basal edge and notch grinding produces a squared-off base effect. Proportionately narrower than the Big Sandy.

Comment: The Raddatz is apparently the earliest of this general form.

26. Simonsen

Age: 10,000 to 7500 B.P., estimated. At Modoc Rockshelter in southwestern Illinois, a Simonsen was found under a level C-14 dated at 9872 B.P. while another was found with an Eden-Scottsbluff assemblage at the Renier site in Wisconsin. At the Simonsen type site in Iowa specimens date at 8421 C-14 years.

Range: The Eastern Woodlands-prairie edge region from Illinois across Iowa and Nebraska.

Detail: 1.75″ to 2.5″ long. The base is usually concave or "yoke." Base and notches are ground.

Comment: Related to the side-notched Big Sandy and Raddatz themes, the Simonsen seems to pertain to a woodland Archaic people who moved on to the prairies to hunt bison. A similar type, the Kessell, is found throughout the East, as far as New York.

23   Dalton

24   Big Sandy I

25   Raddatz

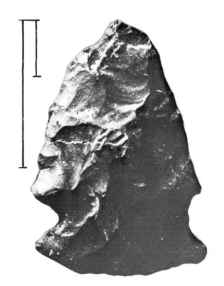

26   Simonsen

27. Charlestown

Age: 9850 (by C-14) to 9000 B.P., estimated.

Range: Upper Ohio valley but the Charleston is almost certainly related to the Pine Tree of Alabama and Georgia. It is named for Charlestown, West Virginia, which is near the type site at St. Albans.

Detail: 1.5″ to 2.25″ long. Blade edges usually serrated. Base is ground but notches are not.

Comment: The earliest corner-notched type.

28. Palmer

Age: 9500 to 9000 B.P. estimated.

Range: East of the Appalachians, from Georgia to New York. Named for Palmer Mt. in North Carolina.

Detail: 1″ to 2″ long. A trimly outlined point, usually with finely serrated blade edges and precise, round corner notches. Heavy basal grinding but no notch-grinding.

Comment: The accurate execution and the heavy basal grinding distinguish the Palmer from later types that resemble it.

29. Nebo Hill

Age: 8000 to 7000 B.P. estimated.

Range: The type site, Nebo Hill, is in Missouri, but the Sedalia of Illinois is almost certainly the same point. The type has a limited mid- to upper Mississippi valley distribution.

Detail: 2.5″ to 7″ long. Thick in cross-section and sometimes weakly shouldered.

Comment: Pertains to a prairie-edge culture, like the Simonsen. It may derive from the Hell Gap-like Rio Grande, though it seems to be much later.

30. Kirk

Age: 8930 (by C-14 date) to 8000 B.P., estimated.

Range: From the Ohio River eastward to New York and southward to Florida and the Gulf.

Detail: 1.75″ to 3.5″ long. No basal grinding. Blade is often narrowed by resharpening so that the shoulders project very prominently.

Comment: Three varieties are recognized: The Kirk Serrated is the earliest and shows close relationship to the Palmer and Pine Tree; the Kirk Stemmed follows and the Kirk Cornernotched is the last variety.

31. MacCorkle

Age: 8900 to 8500 B.P., estimated from C-14 dated association.

Range: Upper Ohio valley, but probably throughout the Northeast, though it appears to be rare. The type site is St. Albans, West Virginia; MacCorkle is a personal name.

Detail: 1.5″ to 2.5″ long. Ground base and notches.

Comment: The MacCorkle appears to be the earliest of the bifurcate base (a deep notch in the base which divides it into two lobes) pattern, of which there are innumerable types: the Pinto, the St. Albans, LeCroy and Kanawha of the Ohio-Kentucky-Tennessee area, the Montell and Pedernales of Texas, the Oxbow of the Plains and southern Canada and W30, W31 and W33 of the Great Basin.

32. Pedernales

Age: from 6500 B.P. to A.D. 500, estimated.

Range: Louisiana to California. Named for the Pedernales River of Texas.

Detail: 2.5″ to 3.5″ long. Those with ground basal edges are probably the oldest.

Comment: Included here because of the apparent extraordinarily long persistence of the type.

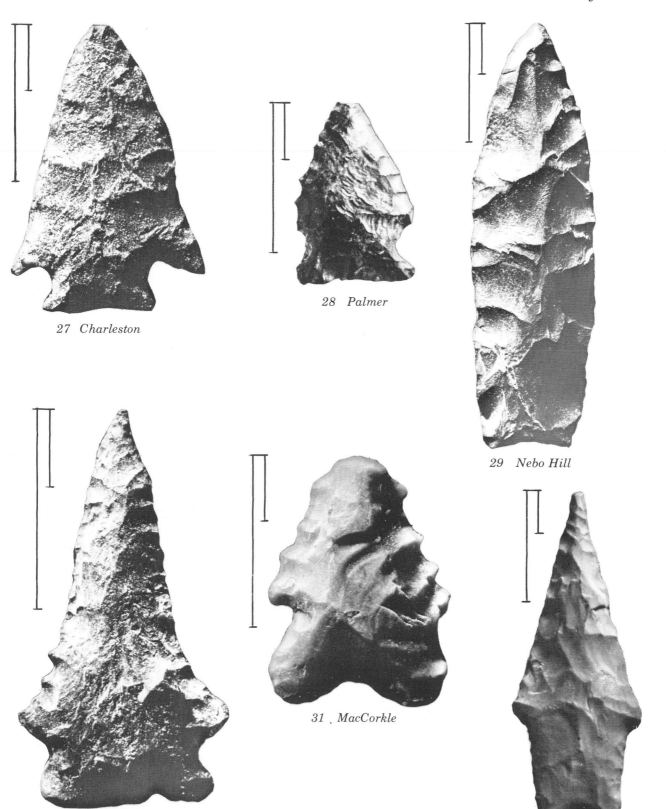

27 Charleston

28 Palmer

29 Nebo Hill

30 Kirk

31 MacCorkle

32 Pedernales

33. LeCroy

Age: 8250 (by C-14) to 7500 B.P., estimated.

Range: Specifically the Tennessee-Kentucky-Alabama-Ohio Valley, but the type is probably widespread throughout the East. The Arredondo of Florida is probably one local variant.

Detail: .75″ to 1.25″ long. The LeCroy is notably small and thin. Many specimens are serrated.

Comment: The question of the relationship of the Pinto of the Southwest and the LeCroy, very similar in striking ways, has not been settled.

34. Eva

Age: 7000 to 4000 B.P., estimated.

Range: The Eva as such is recognized from the Ohio River south to Alabama. The Eva type site is in Tennessee.

Detail: 1.5″ to 3.5″ long. The more recent specimens tend to be smaller.

Comment: Apparently the oldest of the double basal-notched types, of which there are many; the Citrus and Hernando of Florida, the Calf Creek of Arkansas-Oklahoma-Missouri and the Marshall of Texas, all falling approximately in the same time span; the Eshback of the Delaware River valley, of about 4000 B.P. and the Shumla of Texas, not dated.

35. Abasolo

Age: 7000 to 2000 B.P., estimated.

Range: Across the South from Louisiana to New Mexico and into northern Mexico. Abasolo is a place name in Tamaulipas, Mexico.

Detail: 1.5″ to 2.5″ long.

Comment: May be related to the Panamint Ovate. If the smaller Catan type, of the same form and manufacture is a descendant, then this form is one of the longest persisting patterns in the New World. The Catan, probably an arrow point, shows up about A.D. 1.

36. Tortugas

Age: 7000 to 2000 B.P., estimated.

Range: The Southwest, from Texas to desert California, and northern Mexico. Type site is in Mexico.

Detail: 1.5″ to 3″ long. Usually shows one bevelled edge and a large thinning flake in the base, a "pseudo flute." Usually slightly off-center.

Comment: The apparently long persistence of this type, and the Abasolo may be due to the fact that they have seldom been found in reliable contexts.

37. Morrow Mt.

Age: 7000 to 6000 B.P., estimated from C-14 dated sequence.

Range: The Southeast, from the Carolinas to Mississippi. Named for Morrow Mt. in North Carolina.

Detail: 1.25″ to 3″ long. Some variation in the distinctness of the shoulders and the pointedness of the base. Occasional grinding of stem edges.

Comment: Very close in outline and manufacture to the Gypsum Cave, though 1000 years or so younger. This "dwindle" or contracting stem pattern appears in the Almagre of Texas (circa 5000 B.P.), the Gary of the middle South (circa 4000 B.P.) and the Rossville of the Northeast (circa 3500 B.P.).

38. Guilford

Age: 5500 to 4500 B.P., estimated from stratigraphic sequence.

Range: The Piedmont of the Southeast. Guilford is a North Carolina place name.

Detail: 2.5″ to 5″ long. Frequently basally and basal edge ground.

Comment: Like the Nebo Hill, a Paleo-hunter lanceolate tradition-looking point that occurs too late to be in that tradition. It seems to be isolated both in time and geography.

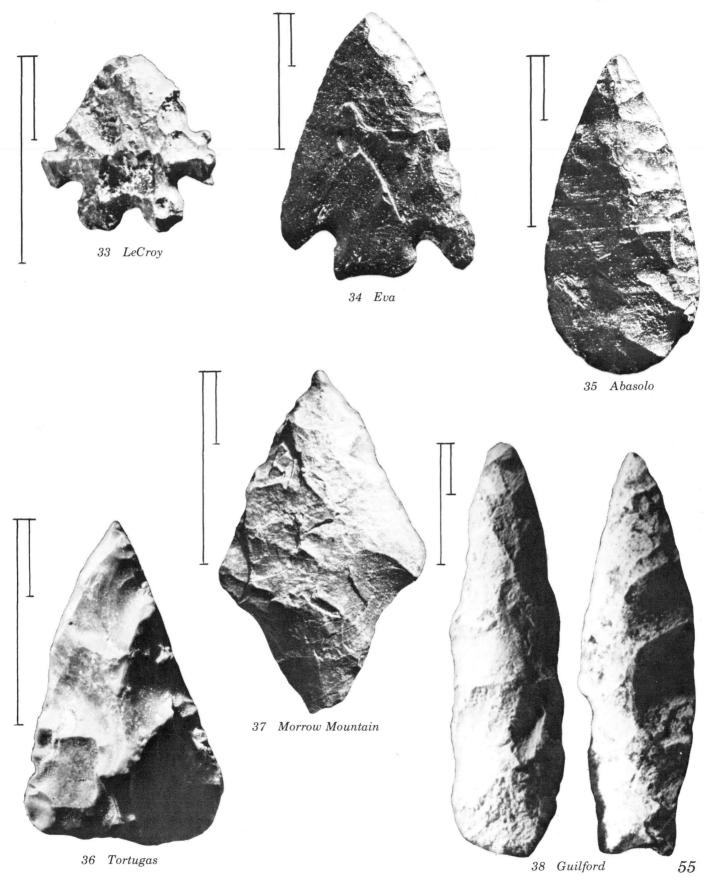

33 LeCroy

34 Eva

35 Abasolo

36 Tortugas

37 Morrow Mountain

38 Guilford

55

39. Friendship

Age: 5500 to 4000 B.P., estimated.

Range: The Friendship is the Ohio Valley (Friendship is an Ohio Valley community) representative of a pattern of usually narrow-bladed, stemmed points that appear all over the East and elsewhere shortly after 6000 B.P. The Lange, Travis and Nolan types of the Southwest are of this pattern, as are the Lackawaxen, the Lamoka, the Wading River, the Bare Island, the Taconic and the Squibnocket Stemmed of the Northeast.

Detail 1.25″ to 4″ long. Broadly flaked, often with the base of the stem not thinned. Usually quite thick.

Comment: Local versions of this simple, sturdy type are to be found all over the United States except the Plains and California. It represents a distinct departure in manufacturing technique from the lanceolates and notched blades and shankless triangles and pentagonals of earlier times. Thinner, more shapely types evolved from the first thick type.

40. Hunterbrook

Age: 5500 to 5000 B.P., estimated, from one C-14 dated occurrence of more than 5135 B.P.

Range: Probably the Northeast and the Middle Atlantic states. It has been recognized so far only in the Hudson Valley. Hunterbrook is a New York place name.

Detail: 1″ to 1.5″ long, with some miniatures about .5″ long. The base is usually ground.

Comment: One of a series of non-stemmed triangles that may have evolved from Paleo-hunter fluted lanceolates in the Northeast, as the Plano lanceolates evolved from them on the Plains.

41. Vosburg

Age: 5500 to 4500 B.P. Several dated occurrences fall within this span.

Range: New York and New England. Vosburg is a New York place name.

Detail: 1.5″ to 2″ long. The base is ground but the notches are too small for grinding.

Comment: The Vosburg is believed to have evolved from the Palmer through a series of subtypes or varieties not yet named.

42. Beekman

Age: 5000 to 4500 B.P., estimated from one C-14 date of 4730 B.P.

Range: Same as Hunterbrook.

Detail: 1.5″ to 2″ long. All three sides are notably straight. The base is ground and, in some instances, the sides are probably ground, then flaked.

Comment: Like the Hunterbrook, very likely evolved from the Paleo-hunter lanceolates.

43. Savannah River

Age: 4500 to 4000 B.P., with one C-14 date at 4200 B.P.

Range: The type name is applied to points found in the Carolina Piedmont (it is named for the Savannah River of South Carolina) and the southern Appalachian mountains, but this big, stemmed style is a member of a whole family of big, stemmed points: the Ledbetter of the Middle South, the Hardin of the Midwest, possibly the Johnson of Arkansas, the Koens-Crispin of the Middle Atlantic area, and the Genessee of the Northeast.

Detail: 2.5″ to 6″ long. The base of the stem is slightly concave.

Comment: This style of very large points seems to appear out of nowhere, with no known antecedents. Its adoption may be associated with a change in hunting practices or concept of weapon manufacture.

44. Merom

Age: 4500 to 3000 B.P., estimated.

Range: The middle and lower Ohio valley, where it is the diagnostic point type of the Riverton culture, apparently very vigorous and long-lived. Merom is an Illinois place name.

Detail: 1″ to 1.5″ long. The Merom is quite variable in outline, comprising stemmed, corner-notched and side-notched variants.

Comment: By contrast with the contemporary Savannah River the Merom is a diminutive point and suggests quite different hunting practices and weapon concept.

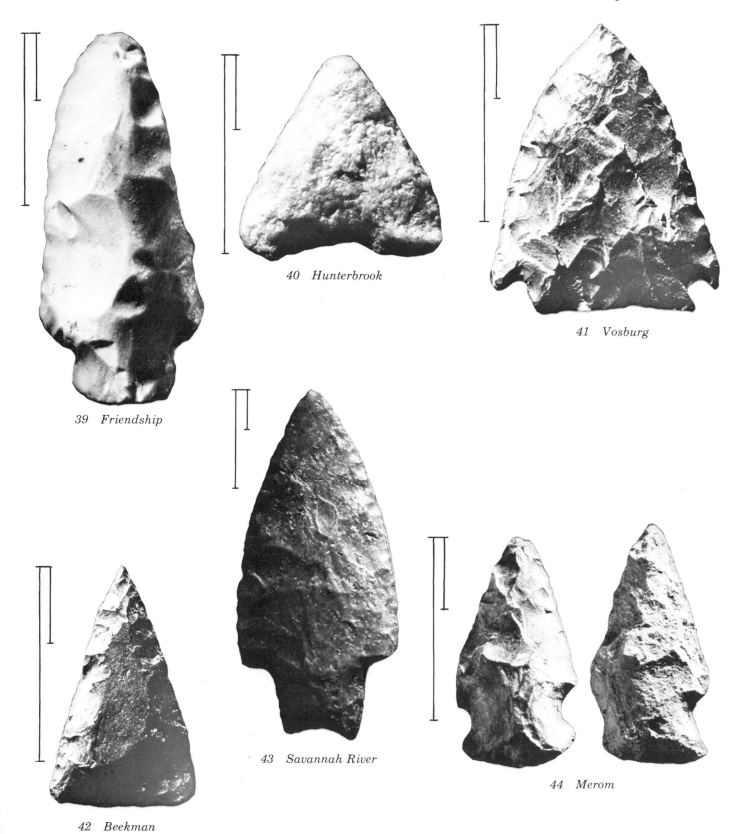

39 Friendship

40 Hunterbrook

41 Vosburg

42 Beekman

43 Savannah River

44 Merom

45. McKean

Age: 4230 to 3630 B.P., by several C-14 dated occurrences.

Range: The High Plains and prairies. The McKean (personal name) type site is in Wyoming.

Detail: 1.25″ to 2.5″ long. Distinctive V-shaped basal notch; no edge-grinding.

Comment: Distribution suggests the McKean was used by hunters of modern buffalo, *Bison bison*.

46. Duncan

Age: 4500 to 3000 B.P., estimated.

Range: Northern Plains and prairies into southern Canada. The Duncan (personal name) type site is in Wyoming.

Comment: Also a buffalo hunter type. The Hanna type is similar.

47. Gary

Age: 4000 to 2000 B.P., estimated.

Range: The southern tier states from Texas to Georgia. The type site is in Texas.

Detail: 1.5″ to 3″ long. Usually not carefully made.

Comment: An unrelated recurrence, apparently, of the Morrow Mt.-Gypsum Cave contracting stem style several millenia later. Contemporary "dwindle stem" styles are the Poplar Island and Rossville of the Northeast.

48. Perkiomen

Age: 4000 to 3600 B.P., on several C-14 dates.

Range: The Middle Atlantic region and the Northeast. Perkiomen is a Delaware place name.

Detail: 2″ to 4″ long. Often assymetric and off-center.

Comment: One of the so-called "broadspears" that, following the Savannah River type, appear in the Middle Atlantic region and into New York. The others are the Koens-Crispin, the Lehigh, and the Susquehanna.

49. Susquehanna

Age: 4000 to 3500 B.P., estimated, on several C-14 dates.

Range: Same as Perkiomen, but the Ashtabula of Ohio is probably the same point. Named for the Susquehanna River of Pennsylvania.

Detail: 1.5″ to 3″ long. The quadrangular blade shape is characteristic.

Comment: A very "stylish" point, almost always made well of good material, more often than not Pennsylvania jasper.

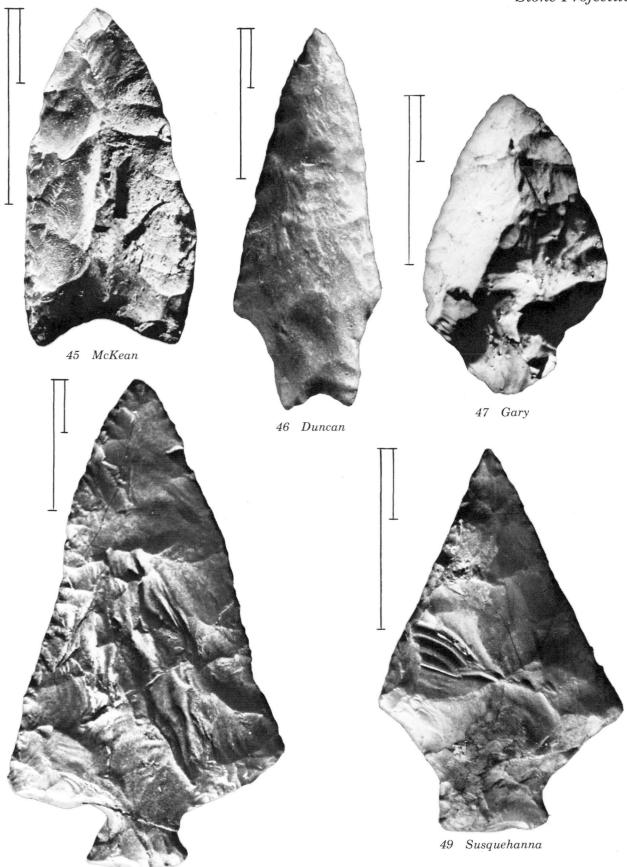

45   McKean

46   Duncan

47   Gary

48   Perkiomen

49   Susquehanna

50. Marcos

Age: 4000 to 2000 B.P., estimated.

Range: Southern Mississippi valley to New Mexico. Marcos is a Texas place name.

Detail: 1.5″ to 3.5″ long. Base usually ground.

Comment: There is a wide distribution of these heavy, deeply corner-notched points over much of the United States at this time level, with the Big Creek type of the Midwest and the Brewerton Corner-notched of upper New York probably related.

51. Table Rock

Age: 3500 to 3000 B.P., estimated.

Range: The Midwest, from Arkansas to Michigan, and from Iowa to Ohio. Table Rock is an Illinois site.

Detail: 1.5″ to 5″. The size range and the proportions, vary considerably.

Comment: A "stylish" point, carefully made of good materials.

WOODLAND (CERAMIC) PERIOD AND CONTEMPORARY TYPES
(Many point types bridged the Archaic into Woodland times.)

52. Fulton Turkey Tail

Age: 4000 B.P. to A.D. 500, estimated.

Range: The Midwest, from Missouri to Ohio, Kentucky to Wisconsin. Fulton is a Missouri place name.

Detail: 3″ to 8″ long. The rarity, size and careful workmanship suggest a special usage.

Comment: The Harrison Turkey Tail can be distinguished as a variety but is very similar. Complete specimens of both the Harrison and the Fulton bring high prices among non-archaeologist collectors.

53. Meadowood

Age: 3500 to 2500 B.P., estimated.

Range: New York, Pennsylvania, Ontario.

Detail: 1.5″ to 3.5″ long. Made by the minimal notching of a thin, biface blade.

Comment: Usually found with the earliest pottery in the area of distribution. Meadowood is the name of an estate in upper New York.

54. St. Charles

Age: 4000 to 2000 B.P.

Range: From Missouri to Pennsylvania, from Tennessee to Wisconsin. St. Charles is an Illinois place name.

Detail: 3″ to 4.5″ long. Like the turkey tails, a type of wide distribution but rare at any one site.

Comment: Known to collectors as the Dove Tail.

55. Orient Fishtail

Age: 3250 (by C-14) to 2800 B.P.

Range: The Northeast. Named for Orient Point, Long Island, New York.

Detail: 1.75″ to 2.5″ long. The stem may be either out-flaring or straight, but the shoulders must be rounded.

Comment: Not all fishtails are Orients; the Orient culture, characterized by ceremonial burial, seems localized on Long Island and the coast of Long Island Sound.

50   Marcos

51   Table Rock

52   Fulton Turkey Tail

53   Meadowood

54   St. Charles

55   Orient Fishtail

61

56. Ensor

Age: 3500 to 2000 B.P., estimated.

Range: Southwest to Southeast. Ensor is a Texas site name.

Detail: 1.25″ to 2.75″ long. A generalized side-notched type characterized by rather cursory workmanship.

Comment: The distribution of this generalized side-notched type seems almost nationwide for this time horizon. Every area, from the Great Basin to New England has its local representative.

57. Adena

Age: 2800 to 2000 B.P., estimated

Range: The territory of the Adena culture, the Ohio Valley from Pittsburg to Cairo, Illinois. Adena is the name of an estate in Ohio.

Detail: 2.5″ to 4.5″ long. The stem is sometimes edge-ground and almost always rounded at the base.

Comment: This type appears early in Adena chronology and is not the only type associated with Adena. The rounded base alone does not make a stemmed point an Adena. It should be long, the blade relatively narrow and the shoulders rounded, with a slight but distinct off-set.

58. Snyders

Age: 2500 B.P. to A.D. 500, estimated.

Range: Mississippi and Ohio Valleys, but a few have been found in northern New York. Snyders is an Illinois site name.

Detail: 2″ to 5″ long. The Snyders is a carefully notched blade of the North type. When found unnotched the North is regarded as a projectile point.

Comment: The Snyders and the North are considered diagnostic of the Hopewell culture, though they are not the only Hopewell types.

59. Pelican Lake

Age: 2500 to 2000 B.P., estimated.

Range: Northern Plains and southern Canada. Pelican Lake is a site in Saskatchewan, Canada. But similar points occur as far south as Kansas.

Detail: 1.25″ to 2.75″ long.

Comment: The Pelican Lake occurs without ceramic association but it is likely that similar points found in ceramic contexts throughout the Eastern Woodlands are related.

60. Waubesa

Age: 2500 B.P. to A.D. 500, estimated.

Range: From Ohio to Colorado, from Missouri to Michigan.

Detail: 2″ to 4″ long. May be confused with Adena points, but are, on the whole, larger and of much wider distribution. The Waubesa site is in Wisconsin.

Comment: A "stylish" point that may be related to the contracting stem Gary. The Poplar Island of the Northeast and Middle Atlantic area may be related.

56 Ensor

57 Adena

59 Pelican Lake

60 Waubesa

58 Snyders

63

61. Cotaco Creek

Age: 2500 B.P. to A.D. 500, estimated.

Range: The middle South. Cotaco Creek is in Alabama.

Detail: 1.5″ to 2.5″ long. Blade edges are often finely serrated or bevelled.

Comment: May be related to the "broadspear" tradition; some specimens are broader than that illustrated.

62. Lowe

Age: 2200 B.P. to A.D. 1000, estimated.

Range: Specifically the lower Ohio Valley, but are probably related to the Steuben of Missouri, the Bakers Creek of the Southeast, and the Chesser of the upper Ohio Valley. The Lowe type site is in Illinois.

Detail: 1.25″ to 2.75″ long. Blade edges and base are often bevelled.

Comment: One of the Hopewell styles.

63. Besant

Age: A.D. 1 to A.D. 500.

Range: Northern Plains and southern Canada. The Besant type site is in Saskatchewan.

Detail: 1.25″ to 2.25″ long.

Comment: The Besant is believed to be related to an expansion of the Hopewell culture influence out of Illinois toward the northwest. Quite similar points appear in Illinois Hopewell sites.

64. Avonlea

Age: A.D. 100 to A.D. 500.

Range: Northern Plains and southern Canada. The type site is in Saskatchewan.

Detail: .75″ to 1.5″ long. The size makes the Avonlea a possible arrow point rather than a spear or dart point.

Comment: The type was used by buffalo hunters.

65. Fox Creek-Cony-
Selby Bay-

Age: A.D. 100 to A.D. 500.

Range: The Middle Atlantic region into upper New York.

Detail: 1.5″ to 3.5″ long.

Comment: The same two associated lanceolate and stemmed forms appear in mid-New York made of flint (the Fox Creek, a place name) in coastal New York made of argillite (Cony derives from "coastal New York") and in Maryland made of rhyolite (Selby Bay, a Maryland place name).

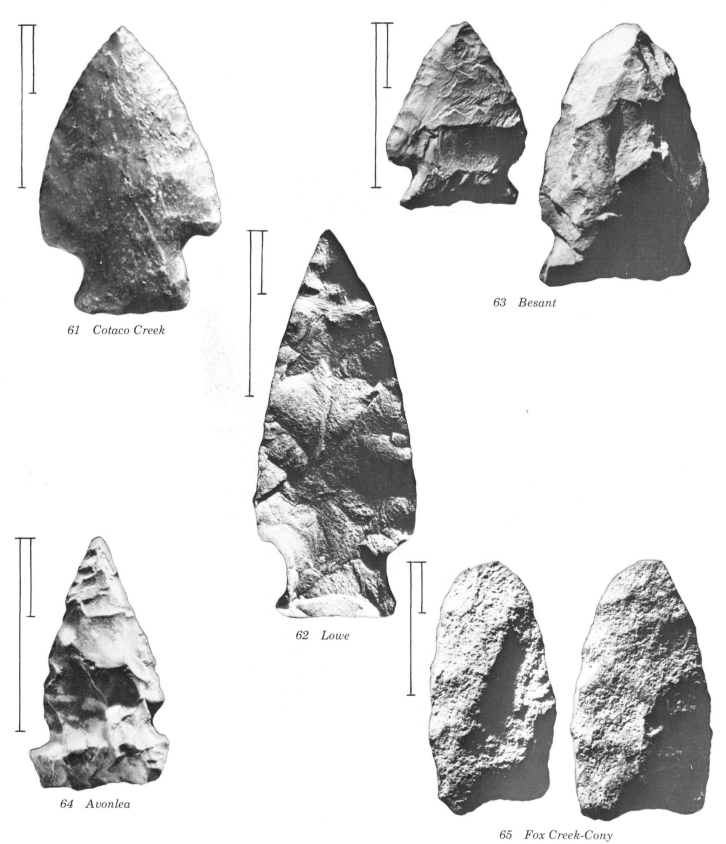

61   Cotaco Creek

62   Lowe

63   Besant

64   Avonlea

65   Fox Creek-Cony

66. Evans

Age: 2500 B.P. to A.D. 500, estimated.

Range: The lower Mississippi Valley and environs. The type was first recognized at Poverty Point. Evans is a personal name. The type persisted after the Poverty Point decline.

Detail: 1.25″ to 2.25″ long.

Comment: Several point types, none of them particularly distinguished, are found at Poverty Point sites, suggesting that the culture drew together many bands or population groups.

67. Copena

Age: A.D. 100 to A.D. 700, estimated.

Range: The middle South. Like Cony, Copena is a made-up name, from copper and galena, the lead ore.

Detail: 2″ to 4″ long. Like the Fox Creek-Cony-Selby Bay, the lanceolate and the stemmed forms seem to be fraternal.

Comment: Diagnostic of a southern Hopewellian manifestation.

68. Vincent

Age: A.D. 100 to A.D. 900, estimated.

Range: The Vincent is the regional Carolina Piedmont name for a series of triangle points that appear about this time, probably related to the spread of use of the bow and arrow, all over the East.

Detail: 1.5″ to 2″ long. It is not good policy to identify triangle points by inspection alone. They need a cultural context.

Comment: Type names for variations of the triangle of the Woodland period include the Yadkin, Uwharrie and Clements of the Southeast, the Greeneville, the Camp Creek, the Candy Creek and the Nolichucky of the Middle Southwest, the Madison of the Mississippi Valley, and the Levanna of the Northeast.

69. Jack's Reef Corner-notched

Age: A.D. 900 to A.D. 1100, estimated.

Range: Northeast, but very similar points have been recognized as far south as Alabama. Jack's Reef is a New York place name.

Detail: 1″ to 2″ long. The very sharp corners at the notch are distinctive.

70. Swan Lake

Age: A.D. 700 to A.D. 900.

Range: The Southeast. Swan Lake is an Alabama place name.

Detail: 1″ to 1.5″ long.

Comment: An unexplained survival of an otherwise obsolete style. It may even be a dart point rather than an arrow point.

More extensive typological descriptions of the foregoing projectile points, and of several hundred additional types, can be found in:

A Guide to the Identification of Florida Projectile Points (Florida State University, University of Florida, Gainesville)

A Guide to Wisconsin Indian Projectile Point Types (Milwaukee Public Museum, Milwaukee, Wisconsin)

A Typology and Nomenclature for New York Projectile Points (New York State Museum and Science Service, Albany, New York, 12224)

Guide to the Identification of Certain American Indian Projectile Points, Special Bulletins 1-4 (Oklahoma Anthropological Society, Department of Anthropology, University of Oklahoma, Norman, 73069)

Handbook of Alabama Archaeology: Part 1, Point Types (University of Alabama, University, Alabama)

Handbook of Texas Archaeology: Type Descriptions (The Texas Archaeological Society and the Texas Memorial Museum, Austin, Texas)

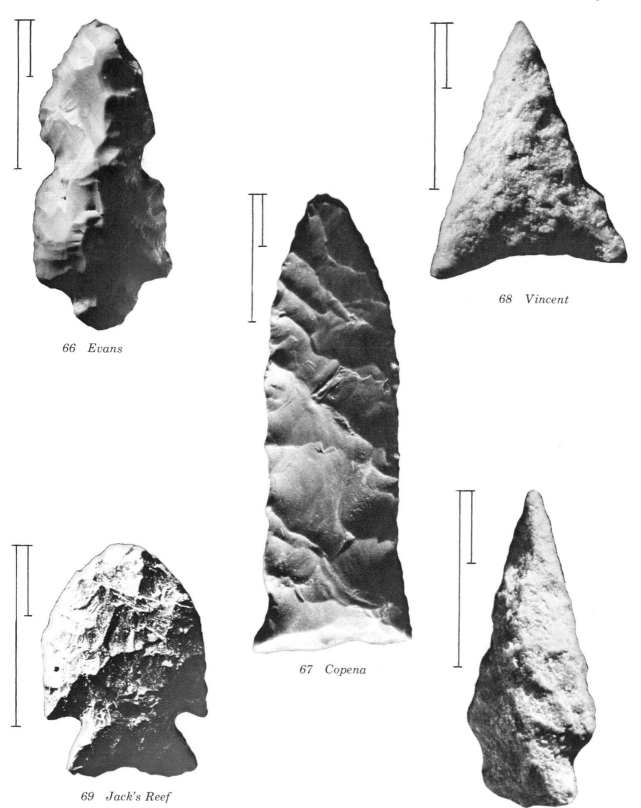

66   *Evans*

67   *Copena*

68   *Vincent*

69   *Jack's Reef*

70   *Swan Lake*

ARROW POINTS

(Usually Associated with Pottery and Agriculture)

| *Catan*
Southwest
A.D. 500
to 1700 | *Alba*
Middle South
A.D. 700
to 1400 | *Perdiz*
Oklahoma to
New Mexico
A.D. 100 to
1500 | *Hamilton*
Southeast
A.D. 300
to 800 | *Huffaker*
Prairies
and Plains
A.D. 1000
to 1500 |

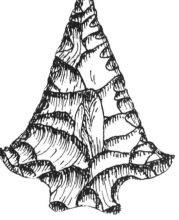

| *Shetley*
Southern Plains
and Southeast
A.D. 1300 to
1650 | *Fox Valley*
Middle West
A.D. 800
to 1600 | *Desert*
Colorado
to California
A.D. 1200
to 1700 | *Madison*
Mississippi
Valley to
Northeast
A.D. 1300
to 1800 | *Cahokia*
Mississippi
Valley
A.D. 900
to 1200 |

chapter 4

Chipped Stone

ADZES-AXES-CELTS

ALMOST ALL ADZES, axes, and celts were made by pecking a core into rough shape which was then smoothed by grinding and polishing with abrasive "rubbing stones." Chipped stone adzes, axes, and celts do occur, however, though it is difficult to identify which is which in the generalized shape more or less dictated by the chipping process. Chipped adzes, axes, and celts probably preceded the polished forms and should be older as a rule than about 6000 years, when the first all-over polished forms appear. In some areas, Florida and certain sections of the Southeast and Gulf Coast, chipped stone adze-celt-axlike implements were made well into the A.D. era, with a corresponding scarcity of polished forms.

BIFACES

The term "bifacial" applies to any piece of worked stone which has been flaked on both sides. A *biface* is any such piece to which the classifier does not wish to apply a more specific designation, such as a knife, chopper, cache blade, etc. The word is used, however, in a special sense in pre-stone projectile point cultures to designate a class of ovoid, leaf-shaped or triangular bifacially worked pieces which may have been used as projectile points and/or knives-scrapers; that is, multipurpose tools.

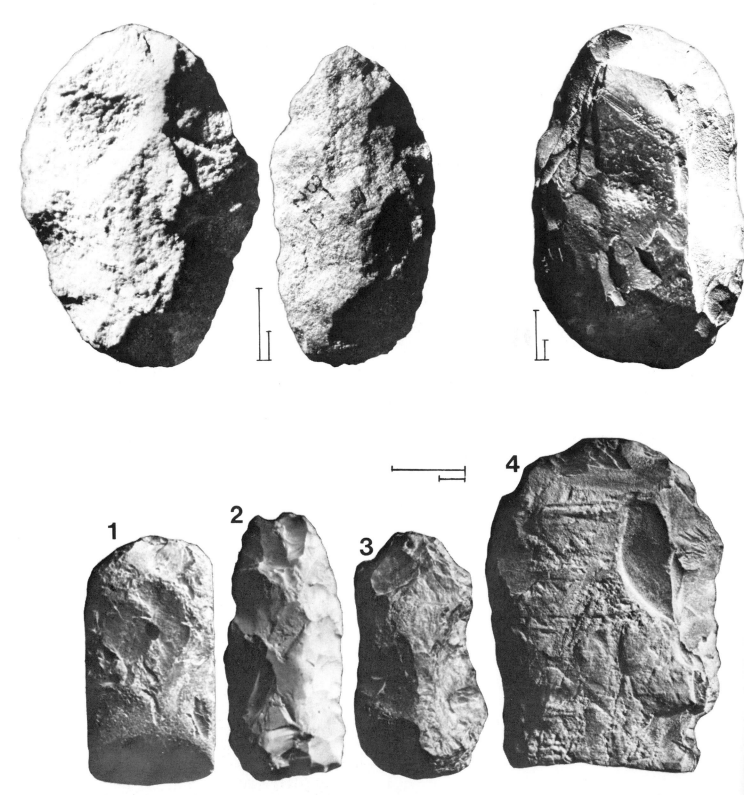

Chipped stone axes–adzes–celts. These seem to be all-purpose heavy cutting tools probably derived, at this stage, from the chopper.

A modern expert in flintsmithing, Errett Callahan, has categorized the stages in stone working thus:

1. Creating the spall, which then becomes the core to be refined.
2. Establishing the edge on this spall-core.
3. Primary thinning of this spall-core and centering the edge; that is, bringing the two edges into convergence at a point at one end.
4. Secondary thinning and generalizing the shape; that is, making the shape bi-symmetrical, in ovoid, lanceolate, triangular or other shape.
5. Specifying the shape; that is, finalizing it preparatory to the notching, fluting or stemming.

All stages from 2 to 5 inclusive are bifaces. Stage 1 may be a uniface or simply a very rough core. Stage 2 would be called a blank, stage 3 a rough blade and stage 4 a fine blade. Stage 5 is the *preform*.

The above stage classification is just beginning to enter the literature.

Stages 1-4 in the manufacture of bifaces by percussion. These are illustrative pieces manufactured by Callahan from quarried Arizona basalt.

A Stage 1 heavy spall, split off a pebble, from excavation.

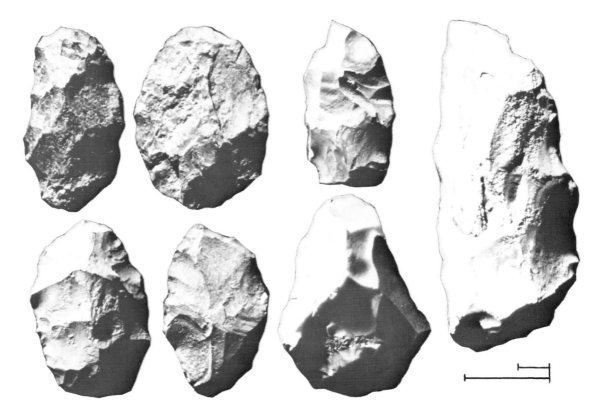

Stage 2, establishing the edge on a pebble blank; from excavation.

Stage 3, establishing the shape: triangular, lanceolate, ovate.

Stage 4, refining the bulk and outline; preforms for a stemmed, a triangular, and a notched blade point or knife.

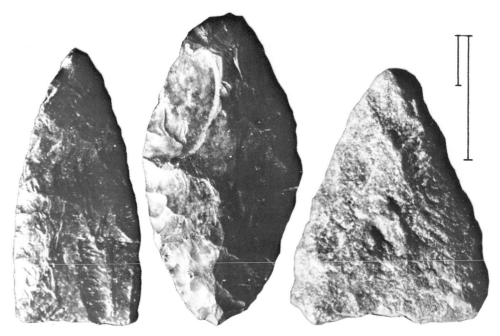

Stage 5, preforms ready for the final notching, fluting, or other detail. The one at left has already been slightly fluted or basally thinned.

BLADES

The term *blade* has three meanings in American archaeology: (1) the elongate, approximately parallel-sided, ridgebacked flake struck from a prepared core and variously called a flake blade, lamellar blade, strip blade or prismatic flake or blade; (2) an ovate, lanceolate or triangular biface, with the designation preceded by a qualifier—i.e., cache blade, ceremonial blade, mortuary blade; (3) the broad, body part of a tool such as a projectile point or knife.

Flake blade. The manufacture of flake (lamellar, strip, etc.) blades has already been explained in chapter 2. In almost all cases the production of flake blades must have been intentional, since it takes a certain kind of blow at a chosen locus on the striking platform to overcome the disposition of cryptocrystalline stones to break conchoidally and thus effect an elongate flake. In most American stone industries flake blades were produced often enough to persuade that they were produced deliberately, but "flake blades do not a flake-blade industry make." In flake-blade industries the flake is the basis for a tool, a small preform, which may be completed with further retouch even, on occasion, bifacially, into gravers, drills, burins, projectile points and knives. What distinguishes the flake-blade industry is the residual core, from which many blades have been struck. The impression one gets from flakes found on non-flake industry sites is that a flake blade was struck from a core whenever the opportunity presented itself during the work on the core to deliver such a flake. On many cores on non-flake-blade industry sites there will appear only one flake scar from a flake blade.

A distinction is sometimes made between (flake) blades and microblades. The distinction may be real in that the dimensions of the blade are determined by the size of the prepared core. Microblades range in width from about 5mm to 11mm with most between 7mm and 10mm; in length they range from 15mm to 45mm, the average being about 32mm.

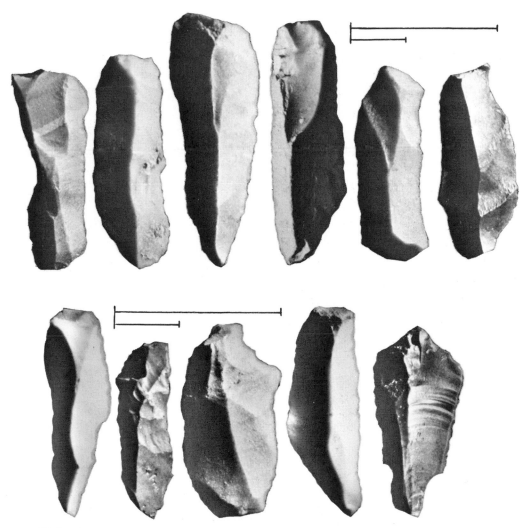

Flake blades. (1) Macro-blades (opposite page). (2) Blades (top). (3) Micro-blades (beneath). Striking platform and bulb of percussion is at top on the reverse side in all instances.

Blades range from 17mm to 60mm in width and 10cm in length. The blade and microblade industries of the Arctic reached the highest level of refinement but this refinement petered out as blade technology travelled south along the Northwest coast. The punched blade technology of Mexico and Meso-America persisted well into historic times. The microblade technology of the Poverty Point culture of the Lower Mississippi about 4000 years ago may or may not have derived from Central America, but probably did. The only other acknowledged blade-making culture is the Hopwell of Ohio and Illinois, circa 2000 to 1500 years ago, but Hopewellian blades were a sort of lithic sideline to a bifacial industry.

To repeat, flake blades may be expected in almost any stone industry, but flake-blade industries are much more restricted in occurrence.

Prismatic blades. While the prismatic flake or blade is a flake blade, the term is more properly applied to those that are thick and triangular in cross section. They make good stock for drills and pointed tools.

Prismatic blades. These differ from flake blades in being thickly triangular in cross section and may therefore be worked on to produce certain tools like the one far left, which has been given a stout perforator tip. Striking platforms at top.

Cache blades. This is not a technological term. Cache blades are bifaces found in caches where they were stored presumably for seasoning and until needed for further work.

Ceremonial blades. The term is used loosely to classify biface blades unusual in size, shape or workmanship, or under circumstances (rare) that suggest their use in non-utilitarian ways.

Mortuary blades. Like the previous two terms, this is also cultural rather than technological. Mortuary blades are those found in graves. They are usually broken, that is "killed" to release their spirits to follow their owner.

BLANKS

The term *blank* is a general one, like biface, applied to any and all of the Callahan stages. But it is coming to mean only quarry blank, the more or less roughly worked biface prepared at a quarry for transport. It is, therefore, not a technological term, though it was once so used, for any of the stages of work between the core and the final artifact form. Quarry blanks become cache blades, or even mortuary blades by being stored or by being included in grave goods. Blanks are sometimes found in graves with stone working tools, apparently identifying the interment as that of a flintsmith or an individual especially noted for stone artisanship.

A cache of biface quarry blades. There were over 200 blades in this cache. They are Stage 2 to 3 bifaces.

A ceremonial blade from a Hopewell grave. Other evidence indicated that the interred was probably a shaman.

Mortuary blades from a red-ocher sprinkled burial. Frequently such grave "goods" or "furniture" are "killed," that is, broken. These are quarry blades in manufacturing stage and may betoken the kind of activity for which the deceased was best known in life.

Two mortuary blades from an Adena grave.

A "killed" or deliberately broken mortuary blade

Two magnificent mortuary blades. The lower blade is 15 inches long. It has been "killed," that is, intentionally broken as grave goods.

Blanks. This general term covers bifaces in manufacturing stages 2 to 5. It is not usually applied to uniface preforms.

BUNTS

Bunts are blunt-edged projectile points for the stunning, rather than the incision-wounding of small animals and birds. It is not always possible to distinguish bunts from certain hafted end scrapers since both were usually made from projectile points broken at the tip by impact. Bunts do not occur in large numbers and are not culturally diagnostic except as the projectile point from used is diagnostic. Most bunts were probably made of wood.

BURINS

The burin is not easily recognized since its working feature, a narrow chisel edge, looks like a sheer break in a piece of stone. It is used for engraving bone, antler, and stone, the same use as the true graver tip. Archaeologists do not accept tools as burins unless the working edge has been produced by a "burin blow," which is the same blow used to produce flake blades but with the difference that the burin flake is very tiny. Outside the Arctic the burin is not a common tool and most subarctic specimens are simple burins, showing only one burin blow. Broken projectile points, since the blade thickness is the right dimension for a burin tip, were often used to produce burins.

CHISELS

Implements with narrow cutting edges at the end of long, heavy, squarish bodies, usually minimally chipped, qualify as chisels and routers. The base is broad and squarish as a platform for pounding with a hammerstone or wooden maul. Useful in woodworking, chisels and routers also served in the quarrying of steatite and the shaping of steatite vessels.

COMBINATION TOOLS

Combination tools are those in which the form includes features or edges to perform two or more functions. A plausible assumption is that these features were combined to accomplish one job of work or production, such as the cutting, trimming, and scraping down of a shaft. The features and edges usually found on combination tools consist of a concave scraper or "spokeshave," a "graver" tip, a short scraper edge, and a knife edge. All of these occur often enough together that the tool on which they occur certainly constitute a class of artifacts as deserving of recognition as knives or projectile points. They should be accorded a name more specific than combination tool but there is no certainty about whether they are one-job or all-purpose tools and any designation given them without certainty might well be a misnomer. There are enough misnomers in archaeology as it is.

The combination tool is often identified by only one of its features and is frequently called either a spokeshave or a graver, depending on which feature is more prominent. But the graver tip and the spokeshave occur often enough in close relation to each other that the two must have been involved in the same operation. Experiments with the "graver tip" found at the corner of Paleo-hunter scrapers have shown that they are probably not graving tips at all but knives, since they rip through hides like razors. Other experiments have found

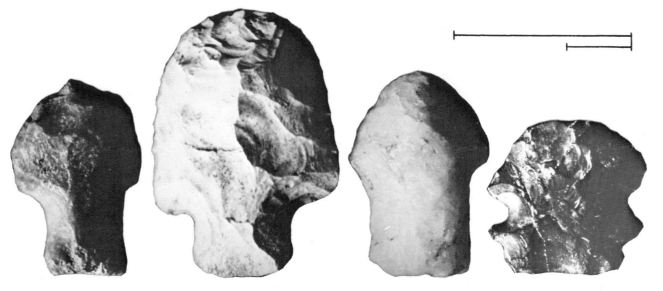

Bunts or "stunning points"

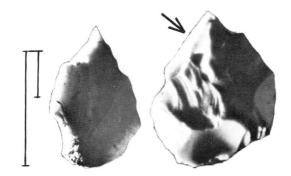

Burins. Note the flake scar of a burin blow on the one at right

that the "spokeshave" performs indifferently as a shaft scraper but works very well as a rotating knife; that is, a shaft can be cut by rotating the "spokeshave" about its circumference, the "graver" tip acting as the cutter. Thus the combination tool is a very subtle implement, but because it was usually made on a flake or discard, an inconspicuous one.

The projectile point form embodies most of the features and edges wanted by Amerind workmen in the execution of their tasks. The tip of the point serves as a punch, drill, reamer, perforator or graver, while one blade edge can serve as a knife and the other as a sidescraper. On some styles a barb at the shoulder serves the cutter function described above for the combination tool and points have been found with a basal "ear" worked into a tiny drill. None of these uses would inhibit the use of the projectile point as a projectile point.

Tools that were obviously made in the form of projectile points but were intended from the beginning as combination tools have been found. They may be called tool kit tools. They have drill-reamer tips, scraper, and knife edges and convex and scraper bases.

Recent analyses of tools found on Paleo-hunter sites in the east by Don Dragoo of Carnegie Museum and Herbert Kraft of Seton Hall University, and in the west by H. Marie

Chisels. They are rough, broadly flaked, partial
bifaces, like choppers.

Wormington, have revealed that making combination tools was a well-developed trait among the Paleo-hunters. The trait must have developed first in prestone projectile point horizons and continued into all subsequent lithic technologies.

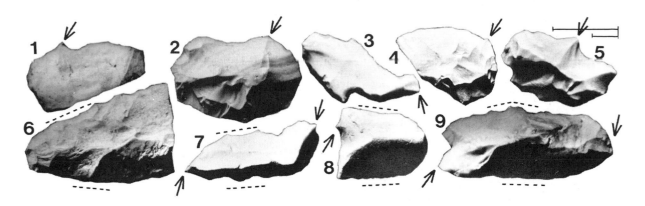

Combination tools. Nos. 1, 2, 3 and 5 show knife edge use, with a "graver" or incising tip at the end of the cutting edge. In No. 4 the graver tip is at the end of a convex used edge. No. 6 is a smooth knife on one edge and a saw knife on the other. No. 7 has graver tips at each end and a concave scraper or spokeshave in the middle. No. 8 has a concave scraper end, side-scraper sides and an end-scraper at the right end. No. 9 has a graver or reamer at the left end, one knife edge, one side scraper edge and a convex end-scraper left end.

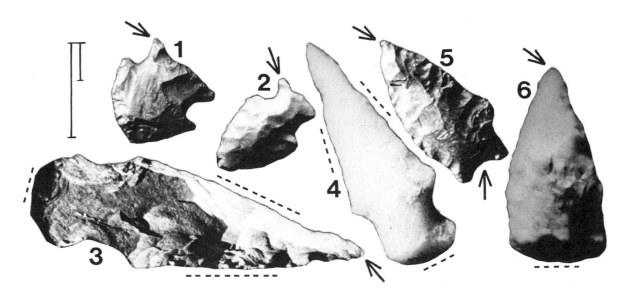

Combination tools on projectile points. In Nos. 1 and 2 the spurs turned upward are tiny drills or reamers, the blade edges showing scraper or knife usage. Nos. 3 and 4 are "tool-kit" tools; the tips are perforators or punches, with use evidence of having been turned in a hole in hard material; the blade edges are knife edges, with one "snag" or graver-like projection on No. 3, and one at each shoulder on No. 4; the rounded bases of the stems are convex end scrapers. No. 5 is a very sophisticated small combination tool; the tip has been used for perforation and/or punching; the left blade edge is a convex knife; the right blade edge is a knife edge with "snag" projection; the concave base is a spokeshave. No. 6 is a double-edged knife with a straight-edge scraper base and a "nose" point.

CORES

The most specific meaning of core is a block of stone from which chips have been removed, the chips and flakes being the wanted product of the chipping. Generally, it is any block of stone from which chips have been removed. Since many of the cores found on sites are pieces which have proved to be intractable in the working or otherwise unsatisfactory for further work, they are more properly rejected cores or rejects. Rejects are ordinarily the spoiled products in core industries, the production of bifacial tools. But cores intended for flake production could also go wrong. The edges of cores were frequently used casually as knives or scrapers and features that developed in the chipping were sometimes accentuated to make a tool that probably had not been initially intended by the maker.

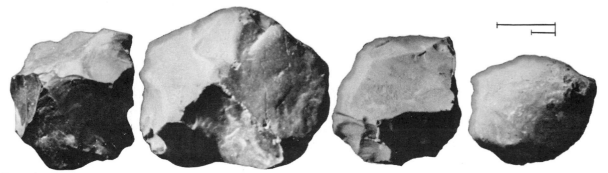

Rough cores. These are Stage 1 pieces made on pebbles. The workman may have wanted only some flakes from them, or he may simply have abandoned them as unlikely to shape up into the form desired.

CRESCENTS

The crescent is an enigma. Found in early horizons, 7000 to 10,000 B.P., it has been called by one authority an amulet, by another a scraper or knife, probably the latter. The region of occurrence is the West, from the Great Basin to California. It seems to be an horizon marker, since it has been found with several different kinds of projectile points, ranging from Lake Mohave and Silver Lake to Scottsbluff-Eden. One crude early crescent has been reported from the Paleo-hunter Plenge site in New Jersey but whether it is a true crescent remains to be corroborated by more widespread Eastern finds.

Rare Eastern crescents

DRILLS

The drill with its long nail-like stock or blade, is instantly identifiable, though some tools that have been called drills are certainly not drills but awls or perforators, or even key-hole knives (see knives). A used drill—and very few unused ones will be found—will have a point rounded from rotation. While there are some "straight" drills that consist of the stock only, most have a broad hafting end for insertion into handles. It has been remarked that the breadth of some of these shanks is puzzling. The handle could not have been as broad as the shank since large handles are of uneconomic motion to rotate. The ideal handle for rotation between the hands is pencil-size. The larger the diameter of the handle shaft, the fewer the revolutions per one pass of the hands. But many drills were made in the prevailing projectile point form, or from broken projectile points, which seems to account for the unnecessary breadth of the shank. But it has been suggested that the blade, in some drills, was not the tool at all; it was the shank, fitted into an antler handle, and the broad base was an end scraperlike tool.

Drills come in all sizes, from tiny ones to drill shell and beads, to the large "twist drills" of the Paleo-hunter.

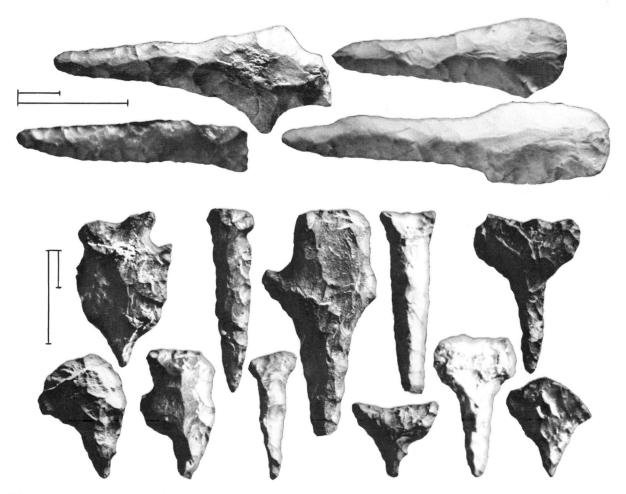

The used drill has a rounded point, from wear in the hole being drilled. The drill wore its way rather than cut its way through the material being worked on. Drilling must have been a tedious process.

GRAVERS

It is the graver tip or spur, not the general form, that marks this tool. The tip or spur is a short, strong protuberant acuity in an edge, usually a cutting or scraping edge. Several such protuberant acuities, not all answering to the precise definition of graver tip, will be described in this section because they are protuberant acuities with uses by artisans who worked with such tools on Stone-Age problems with Stone-Age materials that can only be inferred.

The Paleo-hunters made their broad, steep-edged end scrapers with graver spurs at the corners. No better use has been suggested for these than that already proposed for the graver tips on combination tools; i.e., as slitters or scorers or slicers or cutters of both hide and wood.

Graver tips or spurs.

Other Paleo-hunter gravers are in different positions on the tool and could not have had exactly this use; they must have been perforators, puncturers, or small drills.

But one can think of many functions of piercing, incising or graving, hole enlargement, and lancing that these protuberant acuities could have performed, from boil lancing, splinter removal and tattooing to hole drilling in bone whistles and engraving designs in pottery. More kinds of them are found than the uses that can be imagined.

1. Short, strong, corners or spurs, defined by chipping and/or use, seem suited to graving and the slitting operation already described. They may be called graver spurs.

2. Short, pin-pointed tips seem obviously suited to piercing or pricking, and they might be called pin tips.

3. Longer, needlepoint tips seem made not only to pierce but to penetrate deeply. They may have served as punches or awls, or even as picks to clean out the pith of shafts. A suitable designation might be bodkin.

4. Short, stout noselike projections, either rounded from use or squarish ended, may have been used for jabbing and for enlarging shallow holes. The term nose has been applied to such projections.

5. Thick, heavy-duty beaks on thick-core bodies may be called augers, not because such use is proved or because it differs from reaming, but because the tools were made for heavy bearing-down pressure and use marks show twist wear.

Perforator tips

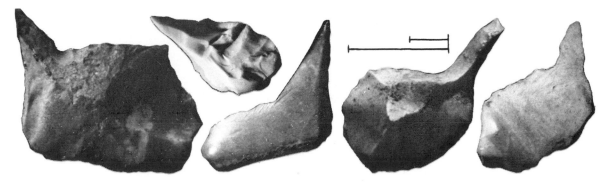

Bodkins. Most bodkins appear on tools that show dual, if not combination use.

"Noses." These appear usually on tools with cutting or scraping use.

Augers. Wear marks indicate that these were turned or twisted in holes of softer materials, such as wood or bone.

HOES

Not all hoes are by any means chipped stone artifacts. Shell was used, as well as stone that would fall into the rough stone category. But certain finished flint blades have been found both in caches in the Midwest and in suggestive associations that indicate their use as hoes. Other types have well chipped edges, though the blade is unaltered platelike rock.

KNIVES

The knife is, functionally, a long run of sharp edge on a "blade," whether that blade be bifacial, a unifacial flake, a spoiled piece, a broken fragment of a tool, or a casual chip. Almost every site of any length of occupation by Amerinds will yield examples of all these knives, formal and nonformal. The edges will show many variations in use, the fine serration of attrition nicks, heavier gouged out edges from hard usage, resharpening retouch by pressure flaking or bevelling, intentional serration for sawing, intentional sinuosity of blade edge for perhaps a somewhat similar purpose. The wear pattern is a series of tiny flake

Mississippian chipped stone hoes. The ovate specimen is a foot long.

Rough stone hoes; Numbers 1 and 2 (from left) were pecked rather than chipped.

displacements—nicks—from the edge, itself, unlike scrapers where the flake scars are along the edge.

There is no inherent reason why a knife edge could not be a scraper and many scrapers would have served as knives, but there is undeniably a large class of artifacts that were solely knives.

Pickup knives. On habitation sites where core chipping was done in camp or near the place of residence, it was apparently the custom to pick up a handful of chips and spoiled pieces with sharp edges to be used for household cutting and once-only use. An amazing number of chips and spoiled pieces on such sites reveal cutting use. The flippant call the spoiled piece knives *ugly knives.*

Chip knives. There can be no doubt that many flakes were struck off deliberately to be used as knives. These usually fall into the flake blade form, although they may not pertain to a flake-blade industry.

Hafted knives. There is no stone industry which produced projectile points that did not use some of the points as knives or make knives in projectile point form. But hafts or shanks were also worked into knife blades.

"D" knives. The designation D comes from the shape, like the letter D. These knives have one straight and one convex cutting edge. They occur in most cultures of the East and Midwest.

Q knives. The Q is for quadrangular. These knives have four straight edges on a rectangle. They seem to occur in the Midwest.

Cody knives. The Cody knife is a diagnostic of the Cody complex of hunters of extinct bison in the northern Plains who made Scottsbluff and Eden parallel-flaked projectile points.

Stocton curves. These slender semi-lunar, serrated blade knives are indigenous to California in late prehistoric times.

Backed knives. These are heavy-duty, one-edged knives usually made on thick spalis. The side opposite the edge is broad, often unmodified pebble cortex, as a hand rest and hand grip. The edges usually show strenuous use. The backing allows the user to put considerable pressure on the grip as he cuts through hard material.

Backed knives are not to be confused with backed blades, flake blades of the same form,

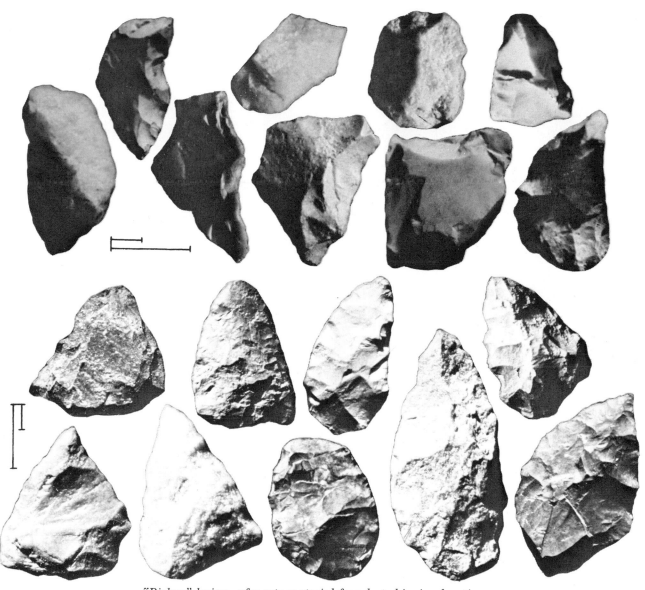

"Pickup" knives, of waste material found at chipping locations.

Flake "pickup" knives. Points and corners also show use.

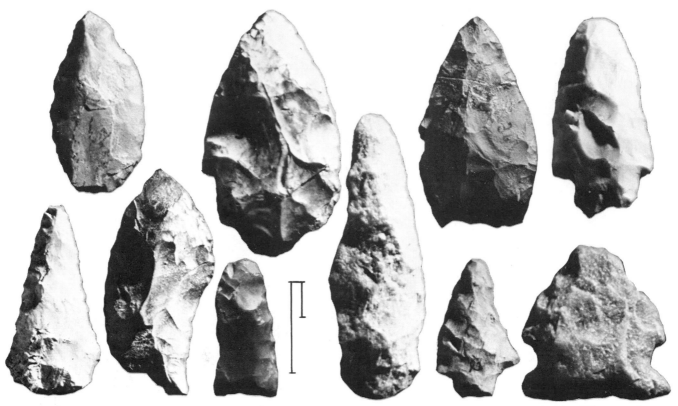

Hafted knives. Most formal knives were probably hafted. These have projectile pointlike shanks. The use of a projectile point as a knife did not necessarily preclude nor nullify its usefulness as a knife.

"D" knives

Q knives

Cody knife

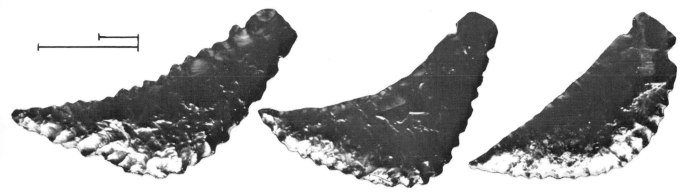

Stocton curves

with one cutting edge and one blunted edge. The blunted edge is sometimes slotted into a shaft or handle as a side blade or it may be used as a finger rest when the blade is used without being set into a shaft or handle. Side blades are usually bifacially chipped and are components of composite projectile points, a side blade on either side of the shaft at the working end, with an end blade at the tip. The composite projectile point is regarded as an Arctic trait but claims have been made that side and end blades have been found in Texas and elsewhere in the West.

Semi-lunar knives. The classic semi-lunar knife, called the ulo (also spelled ulu) is a polished stone implement that is essentially a backed knife with a half-moon shaped blade. It is usually of slate. But semi-lunar chipped knives have been found, though they are rare.

Keyhole knives. The keyhole knife is a narrow-bladed, two-edged knife often mistaken for a drill. It seems to have been used on the same principle as the keyhole saw, that is, it was used to make cutouts within a piece of material, probably hide, without cutting in from the edge.

Biface blade knives. Biface blades, thin and thick, ovate, lanceolate and rectangular, and of all sizes, with knife edge use, are found in most stone-using cultures.

Spoiled biface knives. These are called humpback knives because they consist of bifaces that did not work out because a knob remained on one face after the worker had completed the thinning process. This knob cannot be removed without breaking the piece. When it occurs on the second face worked (if it occurred on the first face the piece would be rejected at that time), the biface already has thinned knife edges. Instead of throwing the humpback away the worker simply used it as is, usually for cutting.

End-stopped edge knives. These are edged flakes and spalls at one end of which there is a graver spurlike projection which stops the straight run of the cutting edge. The meaning or function of this edge stop is not known; it may be a kind of guide to keep the incision in line.

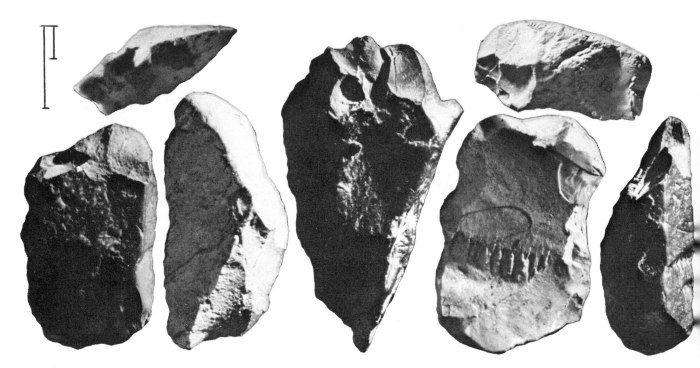

Backed knives

Chipped semi-lunar knives

Inside or "keyhole" knives

Biface blade knives

Spoiled biface or "hump-backed" knives

End-stopped edge knives

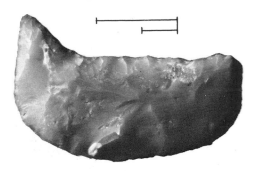

A rare bifacial end-stopped edge knife of flawless white flint

SCRAPERS

The number of tools showing scraper edge use runs into the hundreds of thousands. The commonest form is the pickup chip or the spoiled material piece, but much more deliberate forms were made, maintained by sharpening and retained as valuable possessions.

The four kinds of scraper edges are the convex or arcuate, the rectilinear or straight, the convex, and the hollow. The convex edge is usually found on end scrapers, at the end of the blade's longitudinal axis. The straight edge is usually found on the side of the blade, giving a tool the designation of side scraper. There are, of course, end scrapers with straight edges and side scrapers with arcuate edges and scrapers with both end and side scraper edges; Stone-Age peoples were more concerned with the proper edge than the standard form.

The end scraper was apparently pulled or dragged toward the user from a point of reach in front of him toward him. The side scraper was apparently dragged across the material being worked on from left to right or vice versa. The dragging motion gave a polish to the side in contact with the material, but the nicks of wear came off the edge opposite the side in contact with the material. When the scraper is pushed away from the user it is a scraper plane.

The one chipping technique that is special to end scrapers is snub-nosing, the removal of tiny parallel flakes along the working edge which both sharpened and steepened it.

The concave scraper, or spokeshave, has already been discussed under Combination

Tools. A great many of the features called "spokeshaves" were very probably the rotary shaft cutters postulated. But the task of scraping shafts of wood and bone does seem to have been a probable one and actual spokeshaves must have been made for that purpose.

The hollow scraper has an arched instead of straight horizontal edge. Its most likely use would have been as a spokeshave or shaft smoother, the curve fitting the round of the shaft. Despite this kind of spokeshave and the arguments against designating all concave edge scrapers as spokeshaves, there remains a class of concave edge scrapers with abrupt edges that were probably shaft scraping tools.

The tasks usually assigned to scraping tools are the cleaning of hides, shaping and smoothing and rubbing down shafts of bone, wood, and antler, and smoothing and scraping soft stone, such as steatite, and ceramic pots in process. They were probably also used in food preparation, such as in scaling fish and shredding vegetal fibers.

Convex end-scrapers

Side scrapers

Hafted end scrapers made on broken projectile points.

Concave scrapers or spokeshaves

Snub-nose scrapers. The small ones are called thumbnail scrapers.

Paleo-hunter end scraper with graver spur at corner

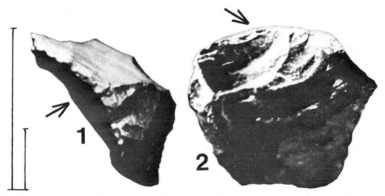

Hollow scrapers. The view of No. 1 is at the curved edge. In No. 2 the curved edge has been made by the removal of a flake.

chapter 5

Pecked, Ground, and Polished Stone

IN THE OLD World the appearance of stone tools shaped by pecking, followed by grinding and polishing to achieve final form and finish, is taken to mark the beginning of the Neolithic and corresponds to the inception of agriculture. No such significance attaches to this innovation in the New World. Nor is there anything to say that the technique was not an American independent invention, owing nothing to imported ideas. The first ground tools seem to be woodcutting or working tools and they show up in the Eastern Woodlands. In time the technique was applied to the production of other classes of artifacts, atlatl weights, plummets, gorgets and pendants, plummets and even, in a limited instance, projectile points. It could have evolved indigenously in many ways, from having to deal with stones that do not flake conchoidally, from the practice of polishing bone and antler, or from observing the polishing effects of the use of stone for digging and woodworking or seed grinding. There is some evidence that the earliest grinding was of edges that had been initially shaped by flaking rather than pecking and that pecking was a later thought. On the other hand, slate, one of the commonest materials used in ground tools, flakes very poorly and does not peck at all. Really good tools can be made of it only by grinding.

ADZES

The adze is a ground stone axlike blade, usually convex on one face and flat on the other used in woodworking, apparently to shape large objects such as dugout canoes, by shaving. The adze is not grooved for hafting but may have been hafted, nevertheless, either in the middle or at the end, like the metal foot-adze. Some adzes were evidently not hafted, but held in the hand and driven, like a chisel or gouge. Northwest Coast adzes were often grooved on one face or had raised ridges for hafting. The working edge or bit will be the width of the blade. Adzes are usually made of igneous stones.

AXES

Axes fall into two general classifications by reason of their hafting groove, the full-grooved and the three-quarter-grooved. The full-grooved axe, the earlier form dating from at least 6000 years ago, is encircled completely by a channel for hafting at a point that separates the blade from the poll, or hammer end. In the three-quarter-grooved axe the hafting groove does not encompass the whole circumference, the top of the axe remaining ungrooved.

Axes vary considerably in the shape of the poll as well as its length and proportion to the overall size. While most axes resemble the metal single-bit ax, with a chopping edge and a hammer end, others have pointed polls, the function of which can only be conjectured. Other axes, with blades contracting to narrow bits, as in the Guilford axe of the Carolina Piedmont, may have been digging or grubbing tools as well as axes.

Ground stone axes come in a wide range of materials, from relatively soft sandstone to tough graywacke and in an equally wide range of sizes, from a pound in weight to ten pounds or even more. What identifies the axe among chopping tools is the groove for hafting and the finely ground or polished bit.

BALLS

While the occasional stone balls found on archaeological sites may in some instances be naturally spherical river pebbles, examination of others will show that they have been pecked and ground into sphericity over their entire surface or over some part of it to remove an assymetry. There is certainly ethnographic evidence that balls were used as club heads in late prehistoric and white contact times but it has been further suggested that balls of earlier times may have been, like the discoidals described later, used in games. The occasional flat facets and random scorings on such balls may be clues as to usage, but they have not yet been interpreted.

BANNERSTONES—ATLATL WEIGHTS

Bannerstone is a misnomer but the term has been in the literature so long that it is ineradicable. What is called a bannerstone is, on the bulk of the evidence, a weight attached to the atlatl or spear-thrower. This "throwing stick" is a shaft or lath-like strip of wood held in the hand and used to launch a spear, technically a dart. The forward or proximal end of the throwing stick, about 24 inches long, is held in the hand horizontally; at the distal or rear end is a hook against which a nock in the dart is fitted. The thrower then casts the dart by

Adzes. The double indentations in the center one may indicate that the handle was attached as in the so-called foot adze, that is, like a hoe.

Full-grooved axes

Three-quarter grooved axes

A Guilford axe, more likely a digging or grubbing tool

Balls; many uses have been conjectured, few have been proved.

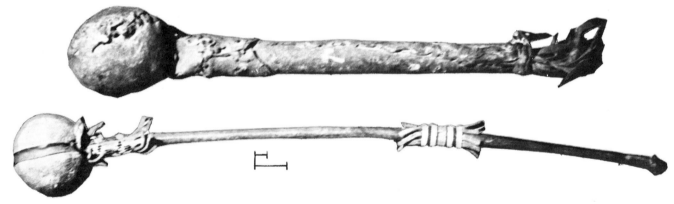

Ball-headed clubs

bringing the spear-thrower forward in an overhand motion, like throwing a baseball. The Atlatl has the effect of lengthening the arm.

According to the late Clayton Mau, who for 2½ years experimented with the atlatl, both weighted and unweighted, casts of satisfactory accuracy can be made to distances of about 70 yards with unweighted atlatls. When a properly balanced weight is added, the distance increases by about 15 percent. Other experimenters, unable to attain the results reported by Dr. Mau, have decided that the bannerstone was used to attain "balance in the hand" of the two components, the atlatl and the projectile shaft.

Dr. Mau obtained best results from an atlatl 23.75 inches long, using a weight of 4.87 ounces attached about 3 inches behind the hand. It was his guess that a younger more athletic thrower could have attained appreciably greater distances than his 80 yard casts. The difficulty that has to be explained, however, is that archaeological bannerstones excavated or collected from aboriginal sites vary in weight from .5 ounce to 1 pound. All of Dr. Mau's experiments confirmed that very precise dimensions were required for optimum results, from the diameter of the dart shaft to the weight of the projectile point.

Only those weights that are drilled through the center to slip on the atlatl stick can properly be called bannerstones. There is a flat, undrilled kind which could only have been tied on to the shaft. That some weights were tied on, however, brings up a question: were there not other kinds of tie-on stones, perhaps those that have sometimes been identified as net sinkers or bolas stones because of their notches or grooves, that could have also been atlatl weights? While recognizable bannerstones and tie-on weights are common enough, they are not as numerous as they should be, considering the supposed universal use of the weighted atlatl beginning perhaps about 5000 years ago. This discrepancy has caused the suggestion to be advanced that the class of artifacts called gorgets, (see *Gorgets*) stone bars with two drilled holes and conventionally thought to have been worn on the breast by strings suspended from the neck, are really atlatl weight forms. Certainly some gorgets would make suitable tie-on atlatl weights but that they are atlatl weights will remain only a possibility until one is found in a grave, beside a skeleton, on an atlatl. This was how the function of atlatl weights was first discovered about 1930, after 50 years of having been known as "ceremonial objects." Some of the weights in the graves where atlatls were first found and recognized were of laminated shell. Bannerstones are easily recognized; other atlatl weights may not be.

Drilled bannerstones decline precipitously west of the Mississippi Valley and the atlatl weight used in the Central and Northern Plains and the Northwest is a generally cylindric form of tie-on, grooved in the middle. In California the atlatl weight seems to be entirely absent, unless a form of "boatstone," rare and unevenly distributed, is such an artifact.

It seems very probable that unrecognized forms of atlatl weights were used before the development of the formalized ones that we now classify as spear thrower adjuncts, since the principle of adding weight and balance to the atlatl would, in the normal course of events, have been discovered and used before the impulse to improve the means of attachment.

BEADS

Stone beads are much rarer than those of shell (which includes wampum discs) of bone, ceramic, and copper, both rolled-sheet and solid. Probably the greatest collection of stone beads in the country comes from the Poverty Point culture. Clarence Webb, describing the content of the Poverty Point culture, wrote in *American Antiquity* (July, 1968):

"Poverty Point beads include long and short tubular, barrel-shaped, globular, disc, and flat or elongate crinoid (fossil) stems. Red jasper and a slightly softer red material (not catlinite, but not positively identified) were favorite materials."

Some of the Poverty Point beads are zoomorphic effigies and must be considered lapidary art.

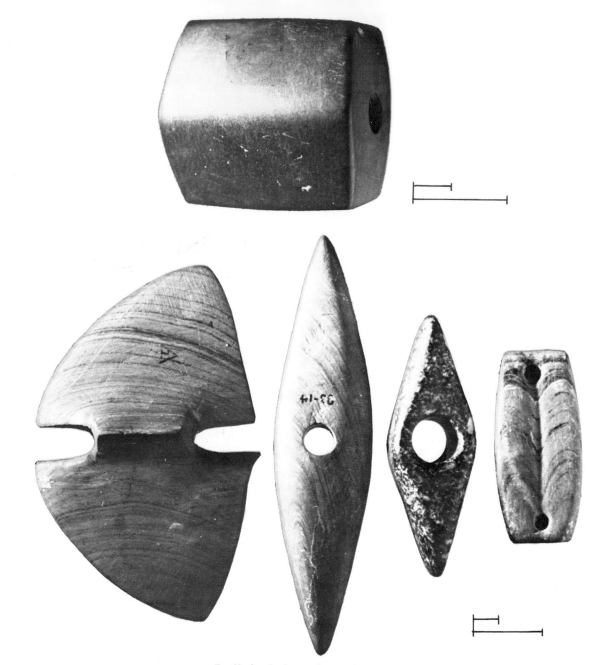

Drilled atlatl weights or bannerstones

Eastern tie-on atlatl weights

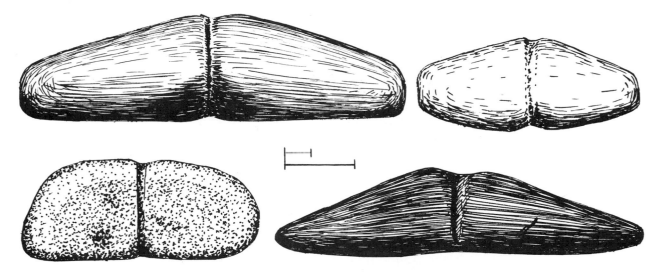

Northwest grooved tie-on atlatl weights

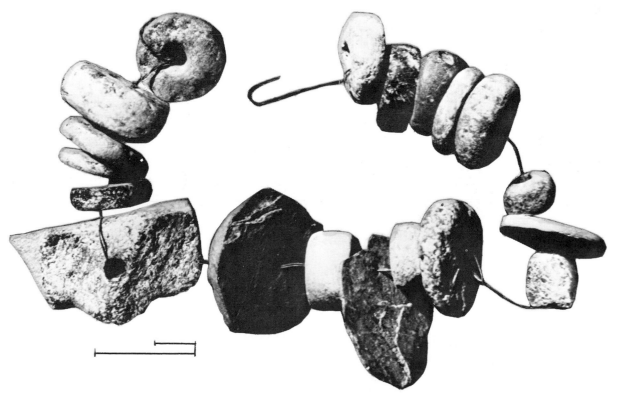

Stone and bone bead necklace

BIRDSTONES

The birdstone is a polished stone artifact that looks like, sometimes naturalistically, sometimes only stylistically, a sitting bird. The most common form is the "pop-eyed" birdstone, with the eyes extrusive from the head. That many of them are drilled with two or four holes has evoked the suggestion that they may have been atlatl weights. While this use is possible they would make awkward appendages to an atlatl shaft. Wherever they are found they are assumed to indicate the spread of influence of the Adena culture of the Ohio Valley of 500 B.C. to A.D. 500. They have been recorded from the Middle South to New England.

The execution of the bird effigy and the drilled holes suggest the wearing of a cult badge, amulet or medicine (magic) object by the owner, but no more than it suggests a clan symbol distinguishing clan authority or preeminence.

BOATSTONES

The boatstone poses the same problems of identification as to use as the birdstone. In plan it is rather like a deep saucer, but in cross section is narrow, hence the name boatstone. It is hollowed out or in some cases channelled or grooved from the top or flat side. It is usually drilled, with two holes through the bottom or convex side, and sometimes with two more holes through the sides at the ends. The channeling and drilling has brought about the suggestion that the boatstone is an atlatl weight but there is not strong archaeological evidence for this use. But then, there is no strong evidence for any other use.

The distribution of boatstones is roughly that of birdstones, and the associations are apparently with Adena-influenced cultures. They do have a kind of superficial resemblance to birdstones in their attributes of drilling, size, and realization of form, but they are not effigies, nor even stylized representations as far as we can detect, and hence probably not cult objects or fetishes.

BOWLS

The manufacture of stone bowls began in the Eastern Woodlands at about 4000 years ago in the Tennessee and Lower Mississippi region. These bowls were pecked and ground out of sandstone and similar workable materials, such as ferruginous quartzite. East of the Appalachians the stone bowl tradition concentrated on steatite; that is, soapstone. The first hard material containers made in the East were of baked clay tempered with grass. This fiber-tempered pottery was found about 4500 years ago along the Gulf Coast and in Florida. It was supplemented there by steatite bowls which apparently were better since they were harder and more durable. Both were displaced by a better ceramic ware, tempered with grit. But the steatite tradition caught on in the Northeast and for 300 to 500 years steatite bowls were the cooking vessels there. Steatite is relatively plentiful all through the East.

The popularity of steatite rests on the fact that it is one of the few stones that can be used in cooking. Most stones, heated over a fire, spall or crack. It is likely, therefore, that bowls of stone other than steatite were not cooking vessels, but mortars or mixing bowls if they were utilitarian, or ceremonial paraphernalia. Few stone bowls are large enough to have been storage containers. Most bowls of stone other than steatite are approximately round, but steatite, easily worked, was shaped into vessels of many shapes, suggesting a variety of uses or at least cooking practices, and into dishes, spoons and cups.

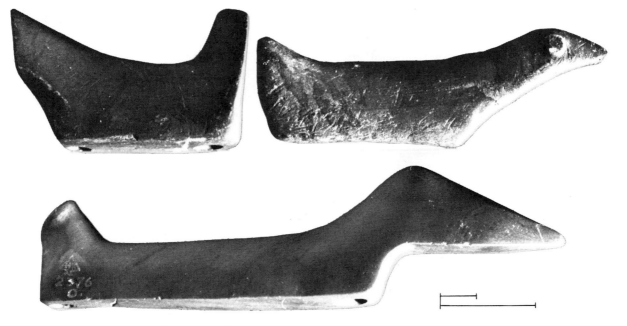

One naturalistic and two stylistic birdstones

"Pop-eye" birdstones

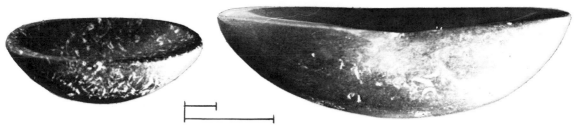

Boatstones; these have holes drilled through the bottom.

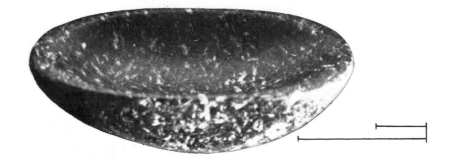

Undrilled boatstone

Steatite (soapstone) bowl

Steatite (soapstone) bowl

Steatite (soapstone) bowl

Western stone bowl of scoria, a volcanic stone

Pecked and ground stone bowl of basaltic rock

CELTS

Celts are usually bi-convex in cross section, with a narrow bit and a narrower after-end. Though they are what we conventionally think of as tomahawk heads they must have been woodworking tools, used like axes in the char-and-cut method of tree felling; that is, a fire was set at the base of a large live tree where the cut was to be made and the celt was used to hack away the charred wood. The process was repeated until the trunk was cut through. In actuality the celt is a specialized form of axe in that it has the axe bit or working edge but no groove for hafting. One known method of hafting was to insert the celt into the split of a live sapling and wait for the handle to grow on it!

CHARMSTONES

If one of the California charmstones were found in the East it would probably be classified as a plummet (see section on *Plummets*). But there is no possible cultural relationship between these pendants and the Eastern plummet. In California they are regarded as fetishes, amulets or medicine objects, with those that are quite phallic in appearance tending to confirm the fetish or hunting medicine interpretation.

CONES and HEMISPHERES

Small cones and hemispheres of polished hematite and galena, ores of iron and lead respectively, appeared in the Poverty Point culture, though the forms are sometimes polyhedral rather than conical or round. Nobody has the slightest notion of what their use was in Poverty Point or in the Adena and Hopewell cultures where they also occur. All three of these cultures shared a general trait of working in exotic materials in ways that can only be called artistic, whatever their production intentions were.

DISCS and DISCOIDALS

Polished stone discs or discoidals are usually classified as game or gaming stones. The best known is the uniconcave or more often biconcave chunkge or chunkey stone used by the Cherokee in the game of chunkge, which was both a sport and a wager game. Chunkge probably had its origin in much less recent prehistory, since discoidal "game" stones appear in inventories all over the United States in contexts back to the Archaic.

In addition to discoidals with concave or dished out faces, discs with flat faces and convex faces are also found. The assignment of polished stone discoidals to the game or gambling game categories is in lieu of any better explanation for artifacts that show no pattern of wear usage. Though some have been called manos, and may be, the identification depends on the presence of the striations typical of mano wear.

EAR SPOOLS

The ear spool is a pulley or yo-yo shaped object of personal adornment worn in pairs at the ear

Celts. Adzes and celts are probably forms of the same basic wood-working tool, though celts have been thought of, and may have been "tomahawk" blades.

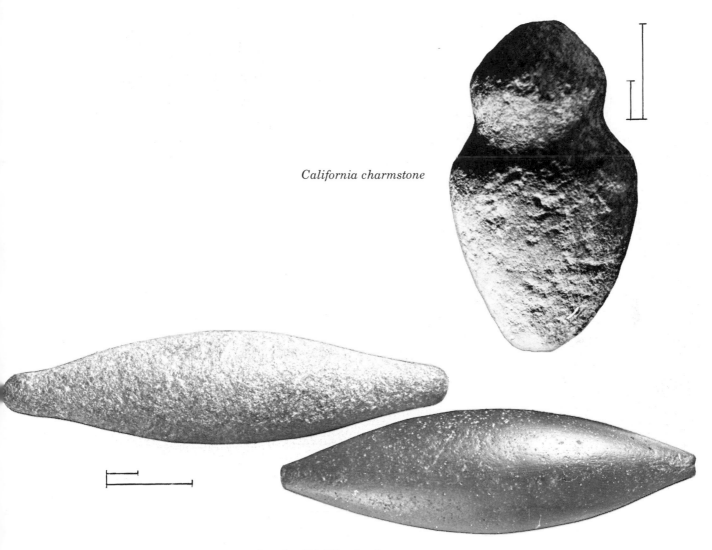

California charmstone

A pair of California charmstones

Hemispheres and cone of galena

Discoidals; these are slightly bi-convex in section.

Discs: the second and fourth ones (from the left) are half polished; the first and third are finely pecked and lightly polished. They are probably gamestones.

Chunkey stone, used in the chunkey game popular among the Cherokees in late prehistoric and historic times.

Grooved discoidals. They would be large and heavy for ear spools.

lobes, like enormous earrings. The ear spool trait appears in the Ohio Valley Adena area, and in Adena-influenced areas at about 500 B.C. and persisted through the Hopewell period, the following Copena period in the Southeast and into the Mississippian period of about A.D. 1100. Ear spools may very well have been caste, rank or prestige symbols.

The earliest ear spools, possibly as early as 3000 years ago, are stone. Later they were made of copper or ceramic, or copper-covered stone or ceramic.

EFFIGIES, FIGURINES and MASKETTES

Effigies, representations of animals and human beings, were probably more carved than polished into shape, but they were for the most part, when made of stone, antler or bone, finished by polishing. Made of ceramic, they were, of course, molded.

The maskette is specifically a facial representation of a human being or an animal, assumed to be a miniature replica of a mask used by shamans or medicine men in their rituals.

Both effigies and maskettes were probably worn as pendants on special occasions, the effigies being clan symbols or charm invocations of guardian spirits or numenistic beings.

Effigies occur in all workable material, in stone, bone, antler, metal, ceramic, and probably wood.

The same figures appear on pipes, as pipes, and sometimes on pottery or as pottery vessels. This category covers only those effigies which are singular as figurines. The figurine-making tradition originated in Meso-America. These figurines are usually female heads reminiscent of the earliest of naturalistic female heads associated with Valdivia pottery, discussed in the ceramic section.

GORGETS

The gorget is a thin, usually rectanguloid polished stone form, with at least two drilled or gouged holes for suspension by strings, believed to be an item of personal adornment worn at the breast. Finds in graves strongly suggest this use. In the "Bannerstone" section the use of the gorget as a tie-on atlatl weight was reported as an alternate possibility. There is nothing in archaeological discovery which will fix the use of the gorget beyond doubt. It may have

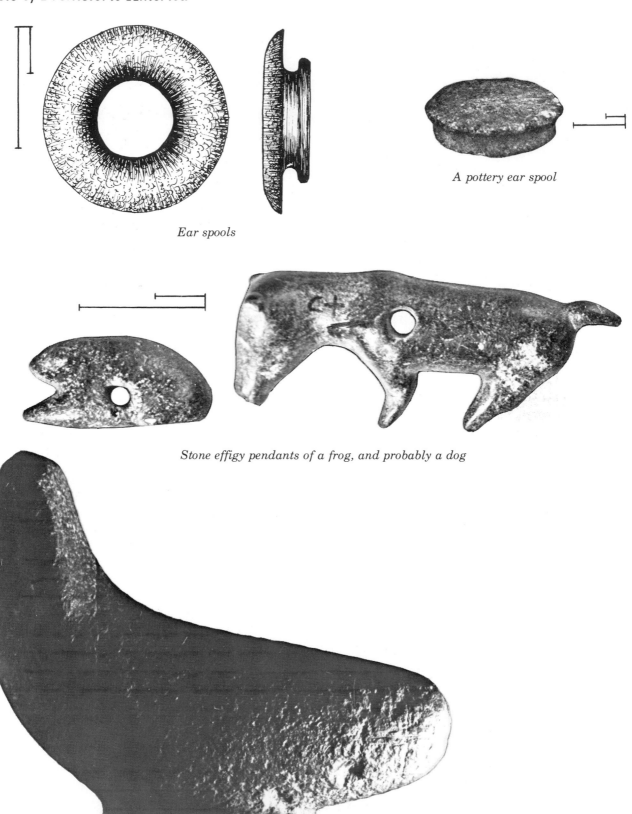

Ear spools

A pottery ear spool

Stone effigy pendants of a frog, and probably a dog

Whale effigy from the North-west Coast

118

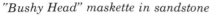

"Bushy Head" maskette in sandstone

Effigy face pecked into a pebble

been an atlatl weight worn suspended from the neck as a matter of convenience, or as a badge of authority, prestige, rank or accomplishment. The two functions are not mutually exclusive. The drilled bannerstone could have been so worn. The term "gorget" derives from a piece of armor worn at the throat which was transformed, after the obsolescence of body armor, into an item of decoration on military uniforms.

Though gorgets are usually rectanguloid, more elaborate forms such as the reel-shaped gorget with two or four hemispherical concavities in the sides were made. Not all gorgets are of stone; one diagnostic type is of shell, and is of sandal sole shape, while other shell gorgets are round and usually design-incised. The latter are late, appearing about A.D. 900.

GOUGES

The gouge is a woodworking implement of ground stone found usually with what is called the Boreal Archaic, a cultural tradition of the forests of Upper New York and New England and adjacent Canada. It has a ground bit, hollowed or curved, and was used apparently to gouge out logs to make dugout canoes. It has a broad, flat platform on the end opposite the bit for driving with a maul, though some were pointed at this end, as though meant to be attached to a wooden base.

Implements that would serve the same purpose as gouges were made of cold worked native copper from Michigan and are found, roughly, in the Boreal Archaic region.

LABRETS

The labret or lip plug is an item of personal adornment, an object shaped like a steel construction rivet worn in a pierced lip. It may be made of polished stone, bone, antler or shell and is found, rarely, on Mississippian culture sites of the Mississippi Valley and the Southeast, and more frequently in Alaska.

MANOS-METATES

The mano and metate are complementary implements used in milling grain into flour. The mano, meaning hand in Spanish, is the grinding stone; the metate, meaning little table, is the nether stone on which the grain was ground by crushing with the mano.

The mano and metate reached the level of formalized implements most notably in the Southwest, where they are related to agriculture. In the Eastern Woodlands area the metate is usually a flat slab of stone and the mano, though it is sometimes a deliberately shaped implement, is just as often a suitable river pebble recognizable by the wear-flattened face of

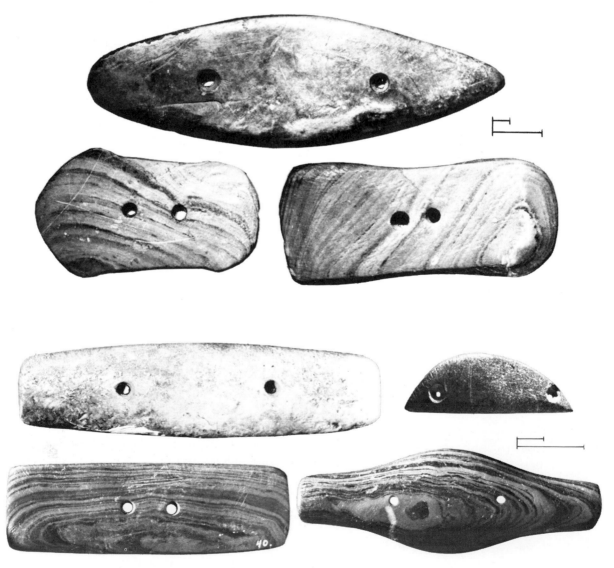

Two-hole gorgets. They could be ornaments or insignia worn at the chest on a string suspended from the neck, or a type of tie-on bannerstone, or both.

Pecked and polished stone gouges

Pecked and end-polished gouge or chisel

Polished slate gouges

A labret or lip plug of gem amethyst

A pair of lip plugs or labrets of shell

the grinding side. Metate surfaces sometimes occur on bedrock outcrops or large fixed boulders.

There is a class of manos that may be properly called combination tools, in the sense already defined of tools put to two or more uses in the completion of one job, by reason of clear evidence of both grinding and hammering. Since these combination manos are usually of softer stones, such as sandstone, it would seem that the hammering was not of lithic materials. Further, the evidence of hammering occurs in patterns, not only on the edge but the sides, which become indented or "waisted." The probability is that seeds were first pounded to break up the tough hulls and then milled or ground.

MAULS

The maul is simply a double-ended, hafted hammer. The implement is not common, probably because a great many mauls were of wood and were not preserved. There is an implement called an axe-maul, with an axe bit and an unusually large hammer end which may be a cultural diagnostic, but it has not yet been placed. Stone mauls are usually found in the Eastern Woodlands, woodworking tools in the Northwest, another region of heavy forests and wood cutting and shaping, being made of bone and antler as well as stone.

MORTARS-PESTLES

The mortar and pestle are complementary grain grinding tools, like the mano and metate. They reach their highest development along the Pacific Coast, though they are also found in the East where they very often occur as small, shallow paint mortars and small, tear-drop-shaped pestles. Many more stone pestles are found in the East, however, than the complementary mortars, the reason being that wooden mortars, made of sections of hollowed out tree trunk, was the most common form.

In the East pestles range from the little paint pestles to specimens two feet long and end occasionally in effigies, which frequently bear heads. West Coast pestles are shorter, rarely more than 8-10 inches in length, for the bowl-shaped mortars, and are more elaborately shaped.

Slab metate and polished pebble mano

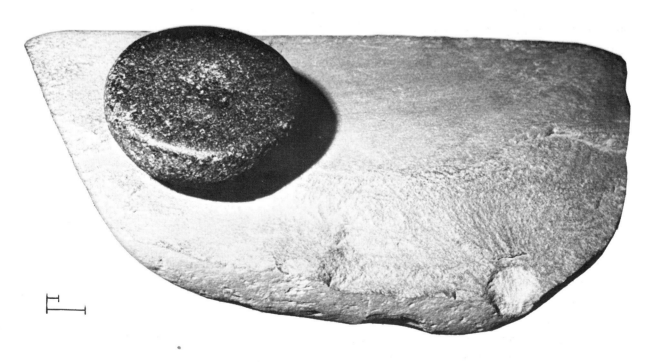

Slab metate and polished discoidal mano

"Waisted" hammerstone manos

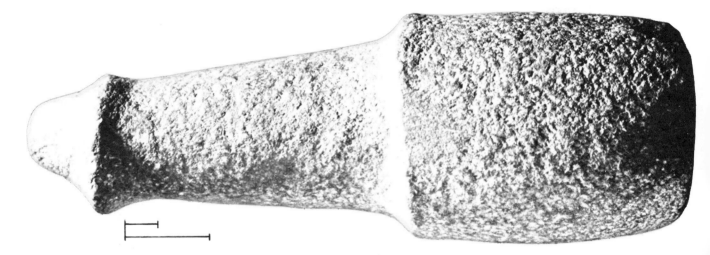

A woodworking maul from the Northwest Coast

Three pebble mauls

Grooved pebble maul

A stone mortar and pestle

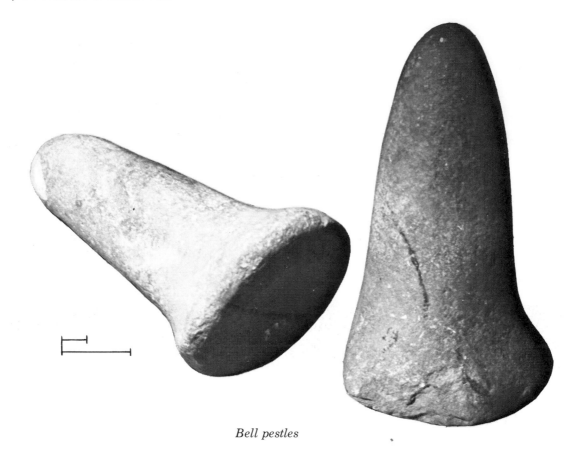

Bell pestles

Partially shaped pebble pestles

A stylized bear effigy head pestle

A phallus effigy pestle

Wooden mortar

Paint mortar for grinding pigments

PENDANTS

The pendant, an item also like the gorget believed to have been worn at the breast by a string suspended from the neck, differs from the gorget in that it has but one drilled or gouged out hole. Whereas the gorget would have hung with its length horizontal, the pendant's length would have hung vertically.

Many pendants look like one-hole gorgets, but pendants are not so narrow a class as gorgets. While many are of polished stone, some are mere holed pebbles, some are animal teeth or pieces of human bone or fragments of stone pipe or even ceramic or stone effigies. Most pendants suggest that they were worn as amulets. An illustrative instance is a stone "bushy head" effigy, with the hole so placed that when worn the face of the effigy looked up at the wearer.

Comparatively infrequent are pendants grooved for the attachment of the necklace string. But several kinds of grooved stones called pendants in the literature appear to be tie-on atlatl weights or plummets.

PIPES

It has been proposed that smoking pipes originated in the shaman's "sucking tube," a hollow bone or piece of antler or wood through which the medicine man drew the evil cause of illness out of the patient under treatment. The medicine man, it is presumed, exhaled the evil spirit from himself after having drawn it out by inhalation from the patient. There is a plausibility about this suggestion, though it hardly seems self-evident. At any rate the first "pipes" are straight tubes, in some instances like the "sucking tubes."

The earliest of these is what Edward Rutsch, of Fairleigh-Dickinson University, in his study of Eastern pipes calls the plain bore tube, a cigar-shaped straight tube with an interior drilled-out smoking chamber. The form may date to 3500 years ago. Though archaeologists generally classify the blocked-end tube, probably Adena in origin, as a pipe, it is a curious one. Made of gray Portsmouth fire clay (or pipe clay) as it usually was, it looks like a piece of old-fashioned lead water pipe, solid on one end except for a small air hole. There is often a pebble in the chamber which acts as a valve at the air hole on exhaling-inhaling. The blocked-end tube varies in length from about 3 inches to as much as 15 inches.

Rutsch classifies stone pipes as: plain-bore tube, blocked-end tube, platform, obtuse angle, stemless bowl of boulder, vasiform or keel shapes, and the calumet, disk or bar base.

The platform pipe is associated with the Hopewell culture of the Midwest, partly contemporary with and partly subsequent to the Adena culture. The bowl, often a zoomorphic (rarely anthropomorphic) effigy, sits vertically on a platform with which it is monolithic. Effigy platform pipes are some of the most arresting artistic achievements of the Amerind. Not all effigy pipes are, however, platform pipes. Many belong to the stemless bowl class, and are effigies drilled to be used as pipes with inserted reed stem.

Stone pipes were made of relatively easy to work stones, steatite, slate, the pipe and fire clays, catlinite and limestone. It is doubtful that many of the stone pipes were personal smoking pipes. The pipes used for the pipe smoking habit, noted by white travellers and visitors among the Indians of the Northeast, were baked clay.

PLUMMETS

The plummet is a ground stone artifact shaped more or less like a carpenter's plumb bob and there is no certainty about its use. Dr. William Ritchie, former New York State archaeologist, who has described the so-called Laurentian phase of 5000-4000 years ago in Upper New York and New England, believes they may have been used as sinkers for fishing lines to which were attached bone or wood "gorges" (see *Bone Implements*) rather than hooks. The plummets of the Northeast, where the Laurentian occurs, are generally grooved at the top.

That there is any relationship between these plummets and those found so abundantly in the Poverty Point culture of the Lower Mississippi of 3500 to 2700 years ago may be doubted. The Poverty Point plummets are usually of hematite or magnetite and are elaborately decorated with incised designs. For the most part they are drilled for stringing, though some are grooved. Since about 2500 have been found, whole or fragmentary, implemental rather than ceremonial use is suggested, despite the decoration. It has been suggested that this implemental use was as bolas stones. Elsewhere they are not found in sufficient numbers to indicate this.

There is a hiatus in the occurrence of plummets in the Middle Atlantic region but it picks up again in the Southeast, with plummets being recorded from Florida in the early ceramic stage. These appear to be utilitarian like the New England plummets, but would more likely be related to the Poverty Point plummets than to those of the Northeast.

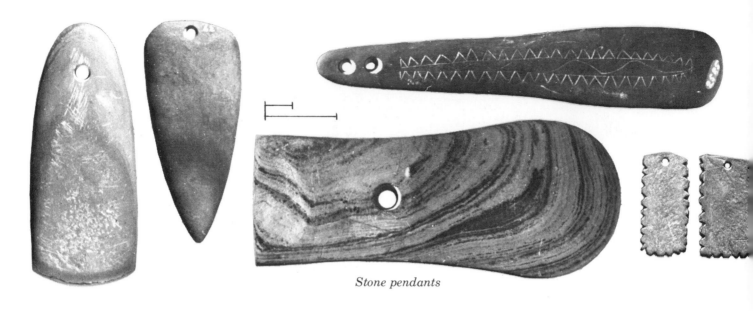

Stone pendants

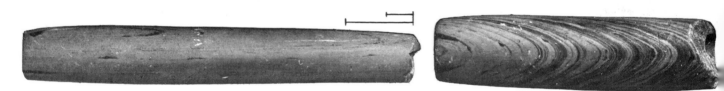

Tubular stone pipes

A Portsmouth pipestone platform pipe from an Adena grave. The bit,, left, shows teeth marks from biting by smokers.

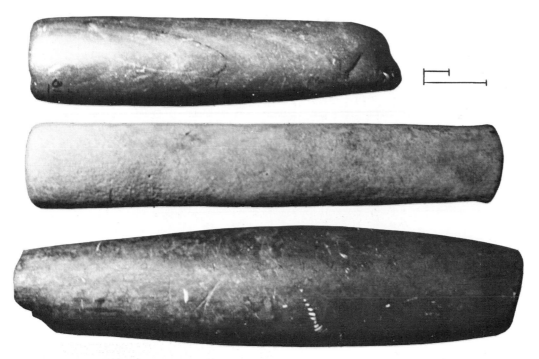

Stone tubular pipes

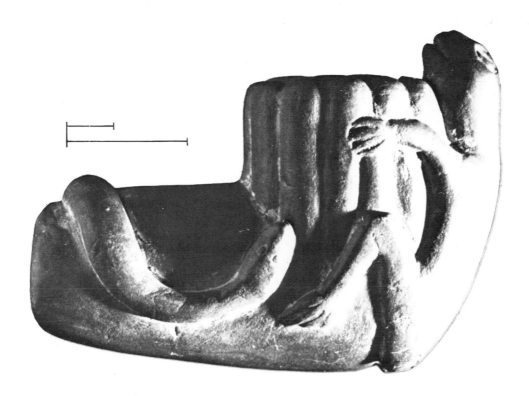

Lizard effigy pipe

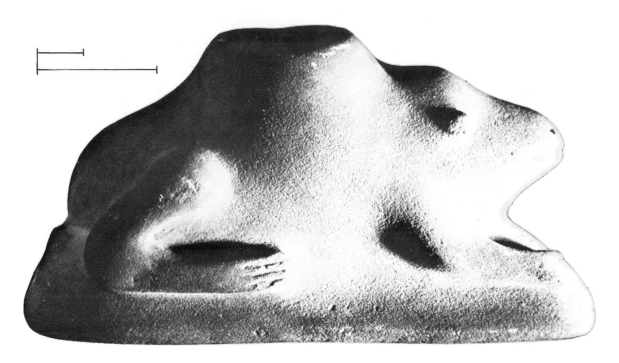

Animal effigy pipe, animal unidentified

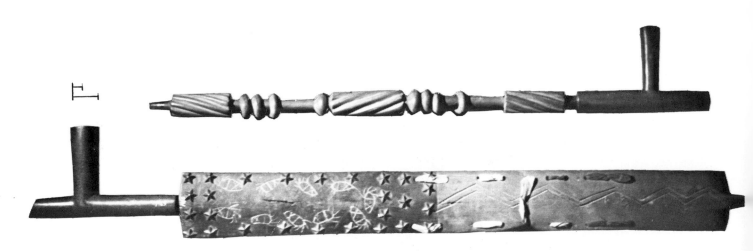

Historic Indian "calumets" with catlinite bowls

Grooved and drilled plummets

PROJECTILE POINTS

There are two centers of the production of ground projectile points, the Northeast—including southeast Canada, and the Northwest including southwest Canada—each of which apparently initiated the trait of grinding slate into projectile and knife forms at about the same time, 5000 years ago. One or both of these centers is responsible for the adoption of the trait of grinding slate by pre-Eskimo and Eskimo cultures which continued into historic times.

These two "ground slate industries" turned out stemmed projectile points and stemmed knives similar to the points, including the formidable "bayonet" points and/or knives, and the ulo (ulu) or semi-linar knife. The ulo is an Eskimo term and the implement is often referred to as the Eskimo "woman's knife." Its origin, as stated above, is not Eskimo, however.

SEMI-LUNAR KNIVES

The semi-lunar knife is almost always made of ground slate. Its shape is described in its designation; it is a half circle, with the working edge the arcuate side and the handle side the straight diameter. While it occurs with ground slate projectile points, as noted under projectile points, its distribution is much wider, from southern New Jersey and eastern

Pennsylvania into New York and all of New England. After the introduction of iron the Eskimo continued to make the ulo or woman's knife, as the semi-lunar knife was called, in that metal. It appears to have been a strictly New World invention.

SPUDS

The spud is an implement, perhaps utilitarian and perhaps ceremonial or symbolic, with a long, broomstick-shaped handle and a semi-lunar blade. The spud is also called a spatulate celt. No study has been done which would demonstrate that the implement is utilitarian, however, and the likelihood is that it has an other than industrial use. The assumption is that it is not an indigenous development but a trait imported from Mexico with the trait assemblage that sparked the Mississipian culture phase in the Lower and later the Upper Mississippi Valley beginning about A.D. 900. The spud or spatulate celt is found only in Mississippian influenced areas.

Polished slate projectile points

Two forms of semi-lunar knife or ulu

A stone spud from the Mississippian

chapter 6

Rough Stone Artifacts

THE CATCHALL CATEGORY of "rough stone" tools includes those tools that were minimally shaped or, like the anvil and pitted stones below, have been used in work that did not require overall shaping of the tool. This does not mean that tool types which have been assigned to the category are not, in some instances and traditions, well made, but that by and large it was the custom to make tools of the type with the minimum amount of work. Many tools in the category have been shaped only by use.

ANVILSTONES—PITTED STONES

The anvilstone is a pebble or slab of stone showing use, in the form of irregular but concentrated pitting, as though it had been the nether stone in an operation in which a hammer or chopper was employed on material held against or on it. But pits or concentrated nicking are often found on the flat sides of hammerstones themselves and even on axes.

The cracking of hard-shelled nuts such as hickory nuts may have caused such pitting, but pitted anvilstones should not be confused with nutting stones in which the holes have been deliberately ground out to fit nuts of differing sizes. Very probably there were several tasks that required the use of an anvilstone.

Another kind of anvilstone, on which the battering shows at the edge rather than in the center, is that found with the Clactonian technology in lithic technology. The anvilstone is a kind of a hammerstone in reverse, the pebble or block from which chips are to be removed being held in the hand and driven against the anvil. Amerinds may have used this technique in making teshoa flakes (see *Teshoas*).

ARROW SHAFT STRAIGHTENERS

Arrow shaft straighteners are flat stones with a single, straight groove running their length. They usually come in pairs, fitting together, one over the other. Experiments have shown that these were heated and cane or reed shafts drawn through them to take out the crooks and joints. Their use, of course, is not restricted to arrow shafts.

BOLAS STONES

The bola or bolas was certainly used by Amerind hunters though the distribution of the weapon is not well documented. In Africa it is believed to be one of the earliest of cast weapons, at least 500,000 years old. It may also have been used by Paleo-hunters in America.

It consists of three or four stones, each attached to a thong the other end of which is knotted to the thong cf the other stone or stones. This central knot is held in the hand, the bolas is (are) twirled about the head like a lassoo and cast at game. The stones spread apart in flight and when the game is struck the effect is twofold: the stones have missle impact and the thongs cause the stones to twist about the legs or neck of the animal. The bolas is said to be very effective against long-legged water birds. Argentinian cowboys use it instead of the lariat to down cattle by entangling the legs.

Bolas stones are usually pebbles with a scoring about the middle and can be separated from net sinkers only after study of the context in which they are found. The discovery of two or three scored or notched pebbles of similar size and weight together would dispose toward their identification as the remains of a bolas.

That form of bolas in which the stones are encased in leather pouches may have been used, but it would have left no clue on the stones, which would not need to be scored or notched.

CHOPPERS

Choppers range in workmanship from pebbles or blocks of stone given an edge by striking off three or four flakes to rather formally chipped shapes. They are hand-held tools, with the working edge usually in one of two positions, on the end opposite the hand-hold, as in hand-axes, or on the side, so that they might more properly be called slashers.

In Old World archaeology choppers made on pebbles or blocks are called chopping tools and those made on large spalls or slabs are called choppers. This distinction is not made in

America, though some of the choppers made on spalls would be called teshoas. The chopper appears at every time level in American prehistory and in most cultural traditions, with spoiled or reject cores often being turned to chopper use.

GYRATORY CRUSHERS

The gyratory crusher is a specialized pod and bean mill of limited distribution. It is described by Julian D. Hayden (*American Antiquity*, April, 1969) as follows:

"The gyratory crusher resembles a perforated mortar, either in slab or block form, in which a wooden pestle with a projection extending through the perforation in the mortar base was gyrated, the projection providing leverage against the under rim of the hole —"

It was used in the crushing or milling of hard pods or beans, such as the mesquite bean. Using a bulbous-ended pestle of wood in a deep stone mortar of light volcanic scoria or tufa, the worker can process the beans into flour very quickly, the flour falling into a basket underneath the hole in the bottom. Two types are known, a deep type and a slab type.

While the gyratory crusher is limited to the mesquite producing area of the Southwest, one other center of use is the Near East, Palestine and Iran.

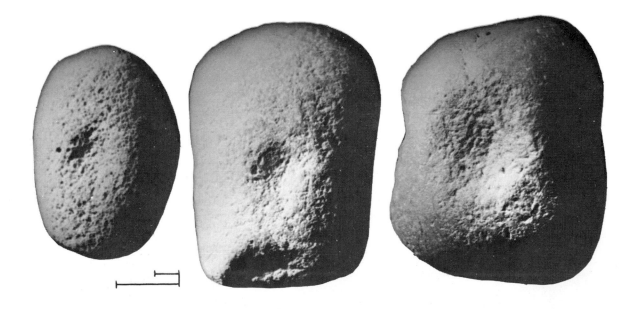

Anvil or pitted stones. The center one is an ungrooved axe with pits on both faces. Such axes frequently are pitted and it has been suggested that the pits were somehow involved in hafting. At far right is a cuboid pebble with pits on all six faces.

Arrow shaft straightener

Bolas stones

Rough choppers

Choppers; at far right is a typical pebble chopper

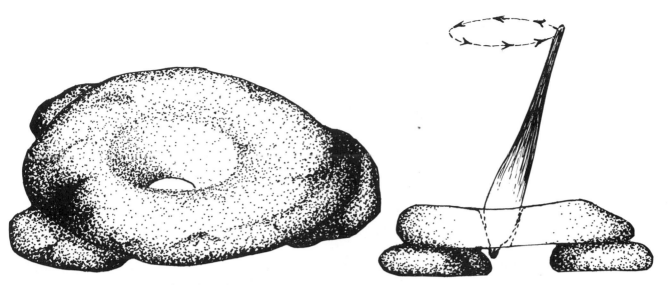

Gyratory crusher grain mill

HAMMERSTONES

Hammerstones are usually pebbles, exhausted or spoiled cores or other lumps of hard stone recognized by the pitting or nicking caused by percussion against other stones or hard substances. The selection of a hammerstone was not as random as it may seem. In flint knapping the weight of the stone was carefully adjusted to the particular phase of the work in progress.

The Indians of the Northwest Coast, however, made hammers for woodworking shaped like bell pestles. Some of these had pointed, conical tops.

Hammerstones long in use will develop a standardized form, such as the disc or the prowed or boat-ended hammerstone.

ROUGH STONE HOES

The chipped stone hoes of the Mississippian era are the exception in hoe manufacture. Most come under the heading of rough stone tools, being minimally worked stones of appropriate shape.

NET SINKERS

Net sinkers are rounded pebbles or flat stones with chipped notches in the sides to hold the net lines from slipping when they are tied on as weights. Needless to say they are found on riverbank sites in some profusion but not on all such sites. Fish were taken in many ways, by hook or gorge, by traps and weirs, and by spearing.

The foregoing description does not apply, however, to a group of net sinkers found in the Great Basin which were either pecked and ground into one of several stylistic shapes, or were items of other use adapted to net weights. Some of these are perforated, some grooved, like plummets, and some notched. Generally speaking, the shapes are hook-like, plummet-like, double-pointed, or shoe-shaped.

Rather carefully worked stones, trimmed by chipping into rectangular or ovoid shapes, with ground notches, are found in the coastal area of the Middle Atlantic states.

Hammerstones come in all sizes, shapes and weights. The evidence of hammer use is a pattern of pitting on the striking surfaces.

Rough stone hoes

Net sinkers

Net sinkers

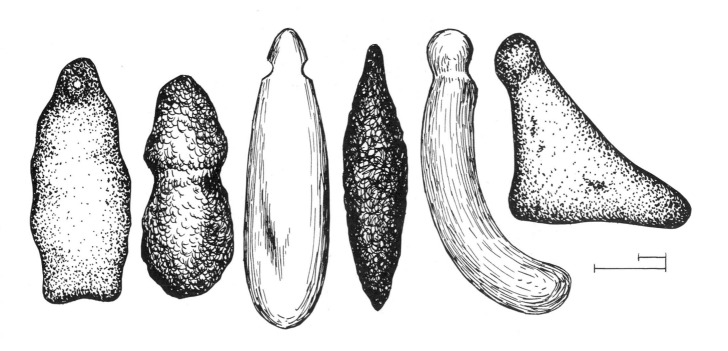

Net sinkers from Nevada

NUTTING and CUP STONES

The nutting stone is a pebble, often a slab of stone, sandstone being a favorite material, in which have been ground small-bore round holes into which it is believed nuts were placed for cracking. Experiments have shown that the proper placement and cracking of nuts, using these holes, opens the nuts so that the kernel can be taken out whole, with no loss of meat.

The term "cupstone" is usually applied to those nutting stones with several holes which may vary in size, as though to accommodate various sizes of nuts. Though some nutting stones were undoubtedly used for nut cracking, it is by no means certain that all stones with "cups" in them were nutting stones. But there are few alternative suggestions.

QUERNS

The mano and metate and the mortar and pestle combinations for the grinding of seeds and grain have been described in the previous chapter on ground stone tools. There is a third combination of food grinding tools in which the handstone conforms in general to the specifications of the mano but the nether stone is neither a metate nor a mortar. This nether stone is usually a cobble into which there has been initially pecked a round depression only slightly larger than the mano. This depression almost immediately takes on the smoothness of polished stone from the activity of grinding seeds and grain with the mano, a selected round or ovoid pebble.

While the combination described is not exactly a quern in the original meaning of the word, the term has been used somewhat loosely for this grinding "mill," and seems appropriate to distinguish the combination from mano-metate and mortar-pestle combinations. This combination occurs most commonly in the Northeast.

STONE RODS

Polished stone rods are found sporadically throughout the country but occur mainly in the Northeast. No use has been suggested for them and they do not show any wear patterns.

RUBBING-HONING-ABRADING STONES

Rubbing, honing and abrading stones had to come in many shapes to fit the kinds of work to be done. Sandstone and other kinds of granular abrasive stones were used to polish, grind, and sharpen both the polished stone tools and other items, such as bone awls and antler tools.

SINEWSTONES

The sinewstone is a flat single or multi-grooved stone, usually sandstone, animal sinews being drawn through the grooves for cleaning.

Cupstones with graduated size holes. The size of some of the holes indicate use for large nuts such as butternuts and walnuts.

A quern or simple grinding mill

Enigmatic stone rods

Whetstones for honing, sharpening and grinding

It is quite possible that the artifacts called sinewstones had other uses or multiple uses. One use that suggests itself is the sharpening of bone and antler for awls and needles by drawing along the grooves.

STRIKE-A-LIGHTS

The strike-a-light is the flint member of the two-piece firemaking kit. The other member is a sulfide mineral, usually iron sulfide; that is, iron pyrites. Any piece of sharp-edged flint will serve as a strike-a-light (as a matter of fact two pieces of flint struck together will produce a spark, but too fleeting to start a fire) but broken projectile points or other pickup pieces were made use of. The Iroquois and their ancestors seem to have made a special form, triangular in shape, with the pointed end stuck into a handle and the broad end used for striking.

The more common way of making fire was the famous "rubbing two sticks together," actually the simple fire drill, rotating a stick between the palms in a hole in a piece of wood called the "hearth." The bow drill and the strap drill were pre-European contact only in the Arctic.

TESHOAS

The teshoa is a flake or spall from the rind of a pebble used for scraping and cutting. It is a very casual tool only occasionally showing any additional chipping. The reason is that the cortex of the pebble is harder than the interior and the unaltered edge was therefore tougher. Large teshoas were used for chopping and digging.

Sinewstones. The multiple grooves may indicate that several grooves were required for some reason to work out a swatch of sinews.

Strike-a-lights. The two at left are pickup pieces of flint; the edges have been heavily battered. The three formal strike-a-lights were probably hafted. They are found only in the Late Woodland.

Common forms of the teshoa

Antler, Bone, Shell, Vegetal Fiber, Wood

THE ARTIFACTS LISTED in this section are all of organic materials. Very possibly the first tools used by man, or proto-man were organic, the osteodontokeratic (a combination of three words meaning bone-tooth-horn) industry attributed by Dr. Raymond Dart to the hominid Australopithicines of South Africa, believed to be borderline men. The effectiveness of tooth and horn in wounding or slaying prey or in defense was an everyday observation by the Australopithicines on their African plains. To use horns and teeth for similar purposes would have simply been intelligent imitation. The very idea of making tools may have derived from the appropriation of these anatomical tools for human purposes.

Atlatl spurs: East of the Coastal Ranges the spur or hook at the distal end of the atlatl, which engaged the butt of the projectile shaft, was made of bone or antler, possibly sometimes of wood. The spur had to be rounded and smooth where it engaged the indentation in the shaft butt so that the shaft would disengage without a hitch. On the West Coast, especially in California, atlatl spurs were made of stone.

Awls: Splinters of bone or whole bones of animals and birds were ground and polished to awl points for piercing and perforating leather and hides.

Baton or billet: The baton, billet or "soft hammer" is a length of antler, bone or wood used as a striker or "percussor" in the removal of flakes from stone. The flintsmith probably used a range of sizes and weights.

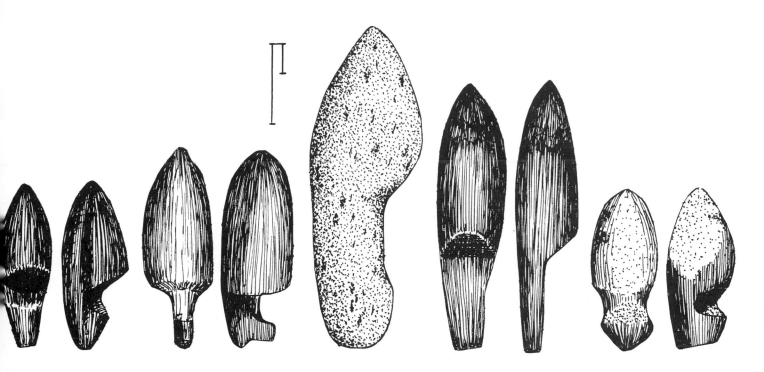

Atlatl hooks or spurs

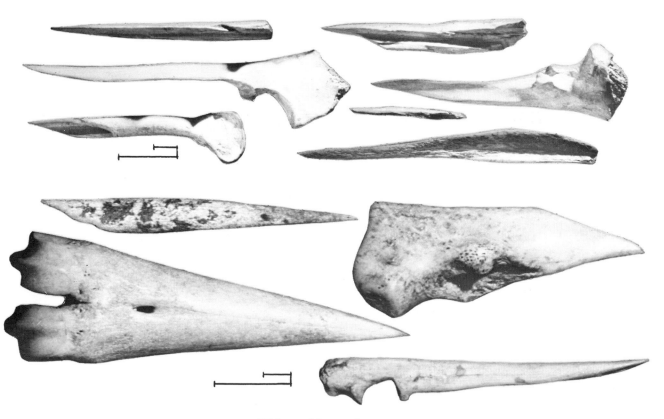

Hide-working awls

Beads: These are of many sizes, shapes and materials—cut lengths and discs of bone; perforated seeds; river mussel pearls; shells such as olivella, marginella and dentalia; the columellae of univalve shells, such as the whelk, cut and ground; perforated crinoid fossils; animal teeth.

Beamers: The beamer is a hide-working tool used to remove hair from hides and to work out the stiffness. It is a simple tool, made usually from the cannon or lower leg bone of deer or antelope, by cutting out a shallow boat-shaped section from the bone.

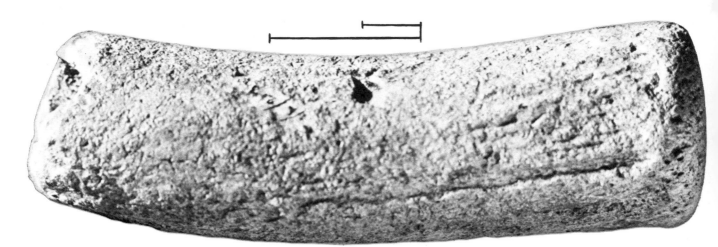

Antler billet or baton for "soft hammer" flaking

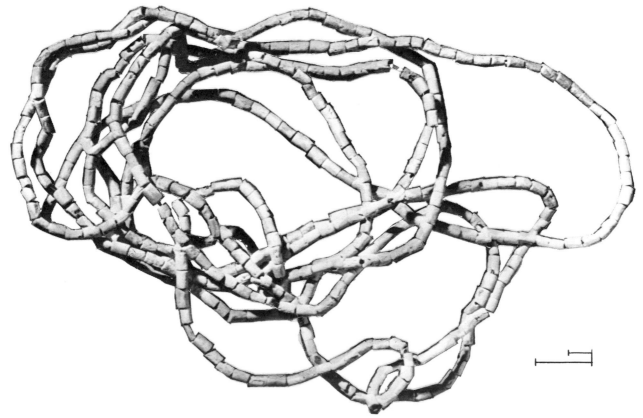

Necklaces of shell beads

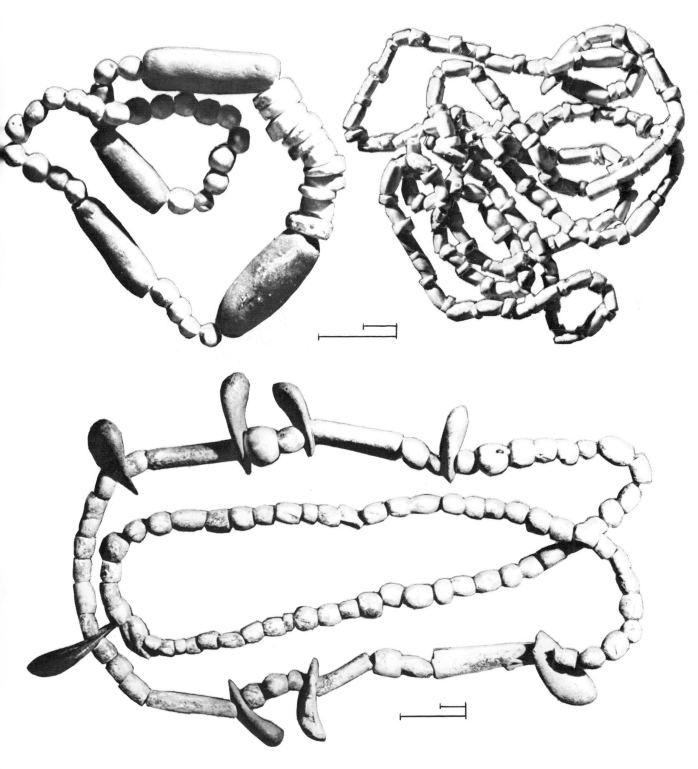

Necklaces of shell beads

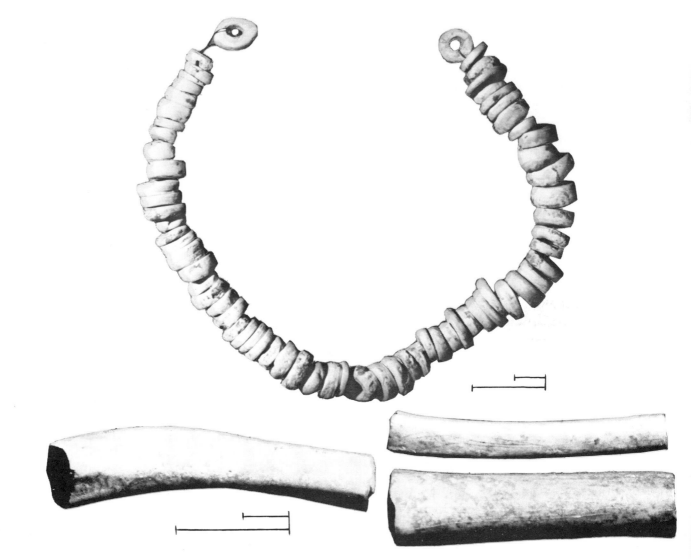

Cut bird bone beads

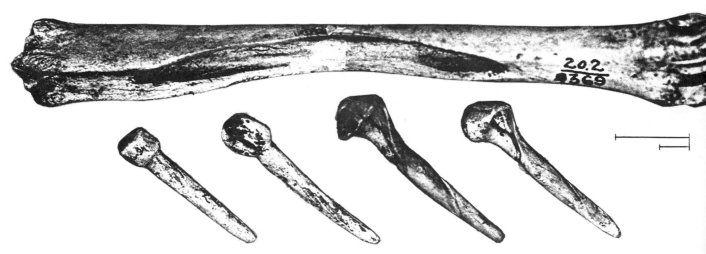

A cannon (leg bone) beamer (above); bone hairpins (below).

A bone beamer. This one has not been cut out as most have been. Note the gloss from use.

Blowguns: The North American blowgun was a simple reed tube for projecting pellets or small, non-poisonous darts with an expulsion of breath, like a beanshooter. It seems to have been used to hunt birds and small game for sport rather than subsistence. Though it may once have been of some importance as a hunting weapon, since it was used over most of North America, it has not survived archaeologically.

Bull-roarer: The bull-roarer is a noisemaking device used by medicine men to create sound effects, and perhaps on other occasions by others for the same reason. It consists of a slat of wood or bone whirled about the head by a string. Some items construed as pendants may have been bull-roarers.

Combs: Toothed combs, often with carved effigy handles, were made, as far as can be determined archaeologically, beginning about 900 years ago. These were made from broad bones, such as scapulae and pelves. Weaving combs were made of wood and few have survived archaeologically. If they had their origin in hair combs, then the wooden hair comb may be much older than the bone comb.

Dibbles: The dibble is a simple pointed stick for digging and for making holes for planting seeds. Sometimes the dibble is weighted with a stone and usually a section of a forked-off branch has been left on the shaft for the foot, so that the stick can be pushed into the ground like a spade. The dibble is known ethnographically only.

Dishes: The carapace of turtles, cutaway conch shells and the valves of large bivalves were used as dishes, dippers, spoons, etc. The chief source of such household items was the gourd. Most of the wooden bowls aboriginally-made come from the Northwest Coast and Alaska and are of contact period provenience.

Ear spools: An unusual form of ear spool made of whelk shell is the long-stemmed kind shown. The discs fit over the ears and the stems were tied together behind the head.

Fish gorges: The angling gorge is a simple bi-pointed splinter of bone slotted or perforated in the middle for the attachment of a line, though the slot was not absolutely necessary. When the fish swallowed the baited gorge a tug on the line set one or both of the points in his gullet.

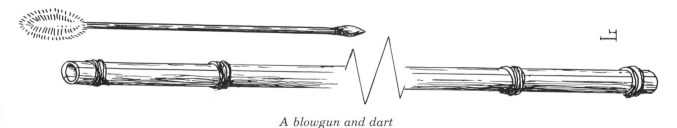

A blowgun and dart

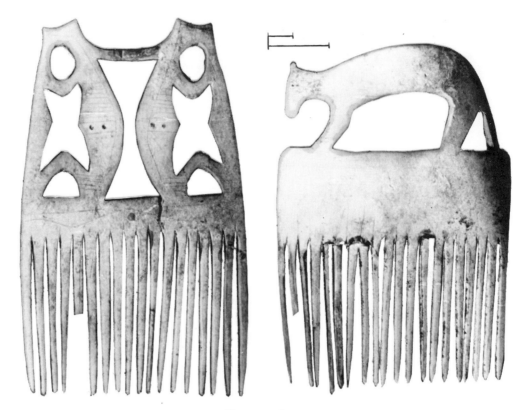

Bone combs

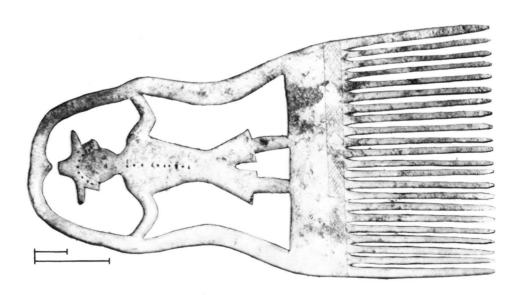

A possibly satiric bone comb of the Colonial period

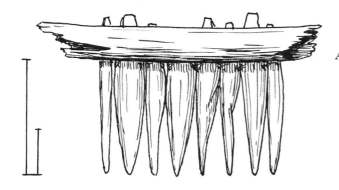

*A reconstructed wood weaving comb from a Hopewell
site*

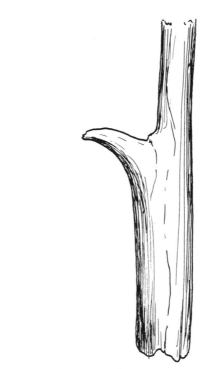

Dibbles or digging sticks and "spades"

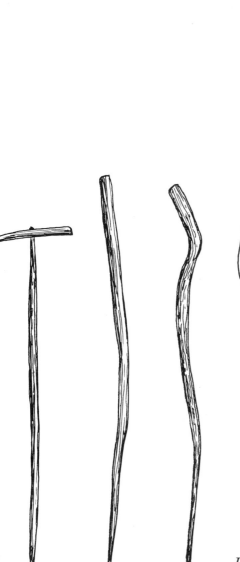

Dibbles or digging sticks of wood

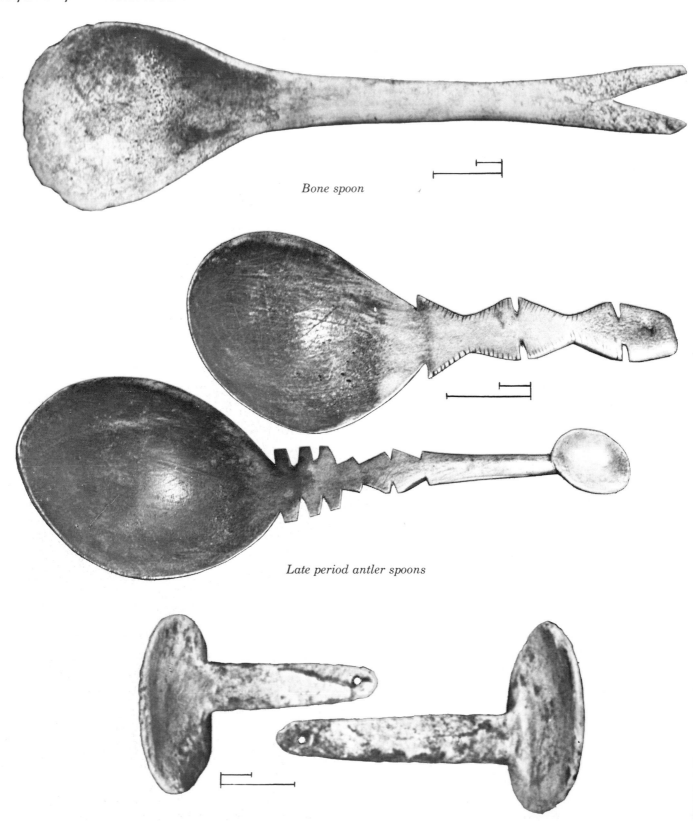

Bone spoon

Late period antler spoons

A pair of tie-on ear spools. Though they are not a matched set they came from the same burial on a site in West Virginia.

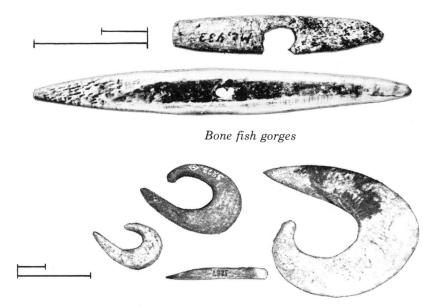

Bone fish gorges

Fishhook from the Northwest Coast and a gorge

Fishhooks: The Amerind fishhook is the familiar J-shaped angling implement usually carved out of a solid piece of bone such as the deer astragalus. But other materials were used that could be made or bent into a hook; in the West a cactus spine was used.

The composite fishhook is a kind of half hook, half gorge. It consisted of a straight shaft attached to the end of a line to which was tied a pointed bone splinter, thorn or sharpened stick. This stick was the hook. Since it was moveable almost any movement during swallowing caused it to lodge in the fish's throat.

Flakers: The punches or drifts used in indirect percussion and pressure flaking were usually of antler, though bone and wood were undoubtedly used on occasion. Modern experimenters have found that these materials are superior to metal punches because they do not slip on slick, hard substances such as flint.

Flutes and whistles: A few flutes and whistles of bone survive; they are usually of typically hollow bird long bones. The stop holes may number from one to five. The Hopewellians made "Pan" pipes of bone or rolled copper.

Gaming pieces: Gaming counters were made of flat discs of bone; dice were made of ground solid bones, like deer astragali.

Gorgets: Most early gorgets were made of stone, as already noted; at least those that have survived were. Beginning with Woodland times they began increasingly to be made of shell, probably because shell was more easily inscribed with the intricate designs that began to appear. With the exception of the sandal sole gorget of shell of the pre-Woodland Glacial Kame culture most shell gorgets are round and some may be classified as pendants.

Handles: While most tool handles were probably made of wood, some antler and bone handles have been recovered archaeologically.

Harpoons: The harpoon head is a weapon point of bone or antler distinguished by its prominent barbs and usually by a line hole at the base. With the harpoon head buried securely in the flesh of the quarry the hunter was able to control it, prevent its escape and

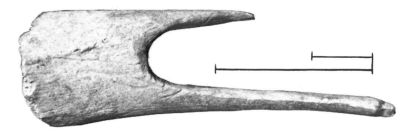

A fishhook in the process of being shaped.

Flakers of bone and antler

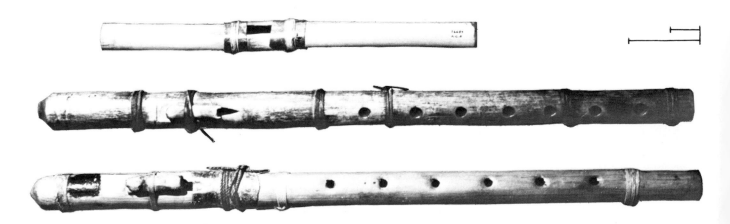

Two flutes and a whistle, all of wood. Indian swains did their courting by playing the flute outside the dwelling of the objects of their affection. Whistles were used for signalling.

A late period Plains Indian flute of pine wood. The insets are catlinite.

The two smaller discs are of polished bone; the larger is of stone. These were found together.

An engraved shell gorget

Engraved shell gorgets

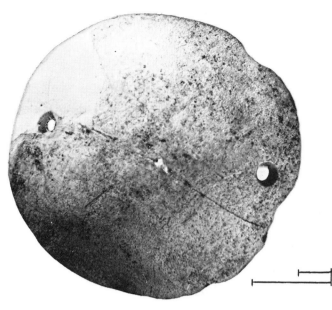

Bone gorget of a human skull cap

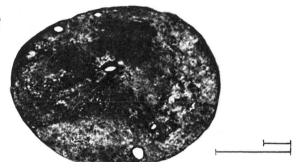

A round Mississippian gorget of shell

Decorated bone handle from the Northwest Coast

Antler hide scrapers. The top scraper has a flint scraper in place.

Flint tools in bone handles

haul it in. The harpoon was used on both fish and mammals, particularly sea mammals. The distribution of harpoons seems to show that they coincide with regions where fishing or sea mammal hunting were of primary importance as food producing activities. They seem to be earliest in Alaska, and appear in the Northeast at about 4500 years ago.

Hoes and spades: Stone hoes and spades have already been mentioned. Other materials used for digging and ground breaking were shells, scapulae of deer, bison, etc., and wood. It has to be assumed that these implements preceded agriculture, having been used to dig the earth from which the earliest pre-agriculture mounds were built.

Lamps: Eskimos, in a virtually fuelless land, used stone lamps fueled with animal fats and oils for both heat and light. One unique citable instance of oil lamps in a region well supplied with combustibles is from Russell Cave, Alabama. Here were found, in an Archaic horizon, two cut bear humerii, hollowed out and showing external signs of having held fire. The fuel would probably have been bear grease. For illumination Indians ordinarily used "candlewood" torches, bundles of any one of a number of resinous reeds and shrubs.

Pendants: In addition to the stone pendants already mentioned ornaments suspended from the neck or ears or parts of garments were made of drilled bear, wolf, elk and other animal teeth, the animals being probably totemic. The Hopewells, who delighted in making skeuomorphs, simulations of items in materials not natural to them, carved bear teeth of wood and covered them with sheet copper.

Pins: One-point pins, with or without heads, were made of bone and antler and used in ways familiar to us as fasteners. Figurine-carved pins are thought of as hairpins, for holding coiffures. A simple device, the pin is probably as old as 20,000 years in America. It may have had multiple uses, such as skewers and picks.

Pottery stamps: Designs on pottery were made in many ways, with netting and other textiles, with combs and with incising points of stone, wood, bone or antler. More complex designs, however, were stamped on with wooden paddles, stone or even potsherds into which the design had been carved.

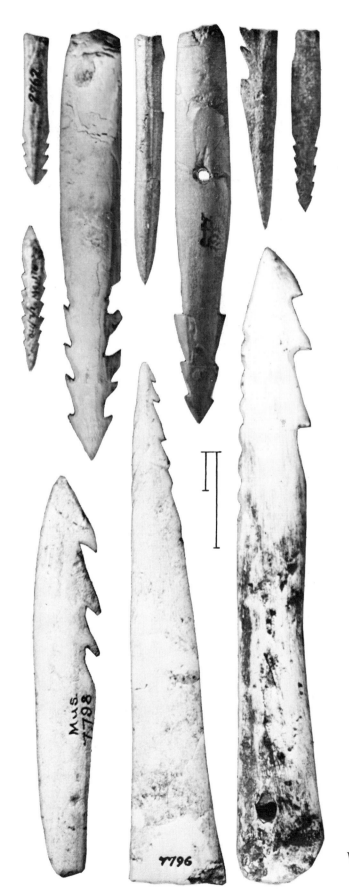

Various forms of bone and antler harpoons

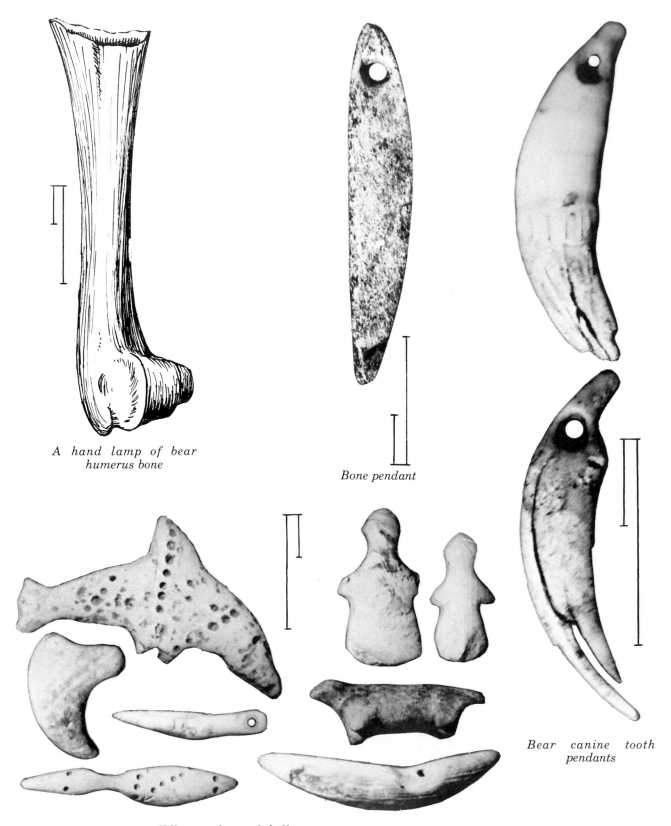

A hand lamp of bear
humerus bone

Bone pendant

Bear canine tooth
pendants

Effigy pendants of shell

Bone pins

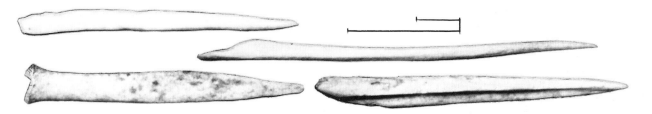

Bone pins, skewers or picks

A bone hairdress pin

Leisters: The leister is a fish spear on the design of the familiar trident of Neptune, used to gaff fish from a boat or the shore. Two, usually three, tines or prongs are set into a base at the end of the shaft with two of the tines, the outside pair in a three-pronged model, being barbed. The tines would be the only archaeological remains.

Masks: While the use of masks in medicine and shamanistic rituals, the wooden False Face masks of the Iroquois and the elaborate masks made by Northwest Coast Indians, certainly must represent ancient traditions, the best archaeological evidence for masks are the maskettes previously mentioned. One of these has been shown to be a miniature of the Bushy Head mask made throughout the Northeast of corn husks. However, evidence from a Hopewell grave has been reconstructed as a leather hood mask, and cut animal jaws, especially of the wolf, are taken as evidence of animal skin masks. The pelt of

A stone "Bushy Head" effigy or maskette

Leister tines

Conjectural reconstruction of a Hopewell leather mask

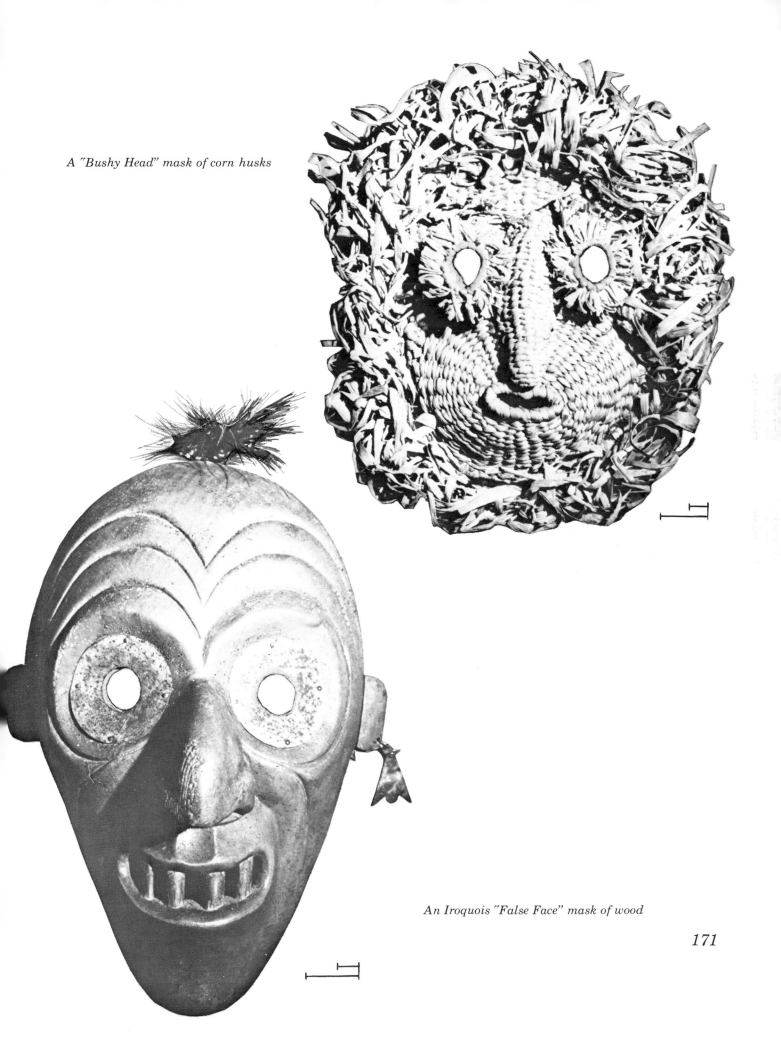

A "Bushy Head" mask of corn husks

An Iroquois "False Face" mask of wood

171

the animal with head attached was worn as a mask, the mandible being cut free so that the mask wearer could manipulate it.

Needles: The age of the eyed needle of bone is in doubt. Apparently it does not go much beyond the Woodland in age, perhaps 3500 years at most. It ought, however, to be much older since the flat netting needle is perhaps 5000 years old. The use was conventional, except in one odd instance. Sinew or a fiber thread was colored, usually with charcoal, and drawn under the human epidermis, leaving a permanent "beauty mark."

Projectile points: Projectile points made of bone were usually simple stemmed or slightly notched forms; probably many were nothing more than sharp splinters of long bones used when a bone point would suffice. The antler point is the conical tip of an antler, sometimes modified for hafting by a hole in the base for inserting the shaft.

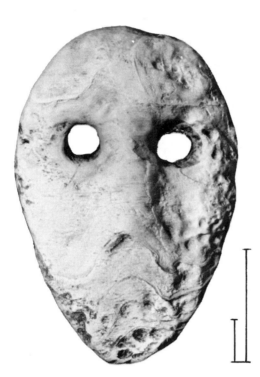

A shell "Bushy Head" maskette

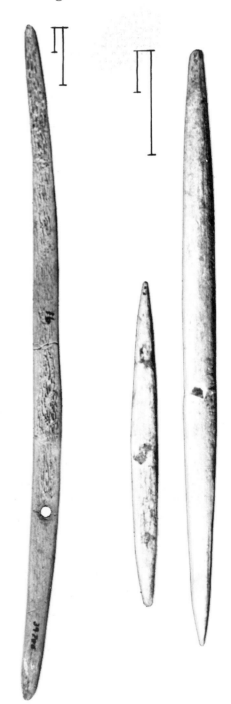

Bone needles; the longer one is probably for net weaving.

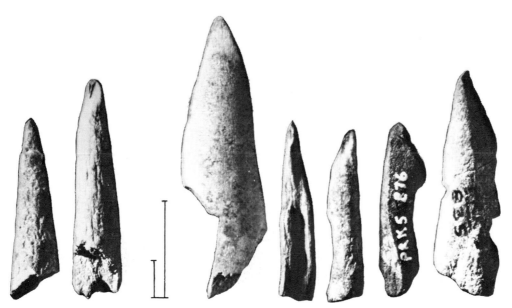

Projectile points of antler (left two) and bone

Rattles and drums: The archaeological evidence for rattles and drums is all from the late prehistoric, probably because of the relatively fragile materials of which they were made, wood, hides and shell. Drums were especially susceptible to decay. But rattles of turtle carapaces, horn and hooves have survived.

Runtees: These are a form of strung bead. They are late and rare. They are coinlike flat discs of shell or bone drilled through the long diameter of the disc rather than the short way, through the face.

Sickles: Grass cutting and grain beheading sickles appear to be late. They appear where grass was cut for hut roofing and other such utilitarian, rather than subsistence purposes. In the West the sickle was made of the split horn of the Bighorn sheep, or of the scapula of bison or deer. In the Midwest the mandible of a deer, teeth in place, was hafted for scything use. (Among the Iroquois the same implement was used for corn shelling.)

Slings: Despite scant archaeological evidence it is believed that the sling, the pouch and thong type used by David so fatally against Goliath, is an ancient weapon, used in both hunting and warfare. About its effectiveness there can be no doubt. Companies of slingers were attached to armies in Alexander's time and played significant roles in military tactics well into Roman times. In late prehistoric times in America the sling fell to the status of what the rubber band sling is today, a boy's weapon. Archaeologically the evidence for its use cannot be decisive; the missiles are pebbles, not marked in any way, as are bolas stones.

Trumpets: The conch shell, with a mouth hole for blowing has been found in grave mounds and other circumstances that suggest its use as a trumpet, like Triton's horn. Some large stone "cloudblower" pipes with special throats have been discovered to give off trumpetlike sounds when blown. These pipes, however, have also been proved to provide copious clouds of smoke, as required by medicine ceremonies.

Textiles and basketry: Textiles and basketry are not common archaeological finds since they are made of fragile vegetal fibers, grass, bast (inner bark of trees and shrubs),

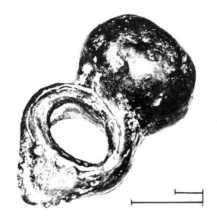

A pottery rattle. The bulbous end is the rattle. Pebbles are used to do the rattling.

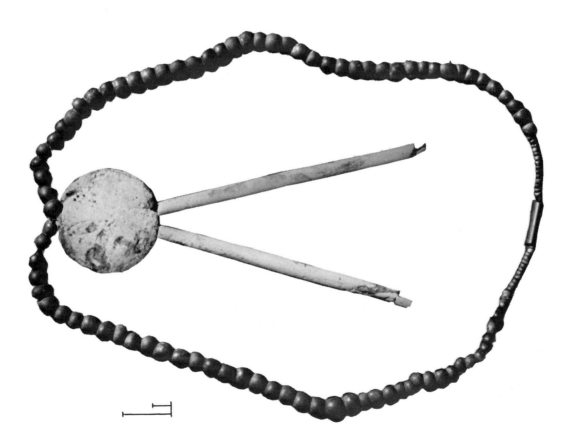

Runtee in necklace

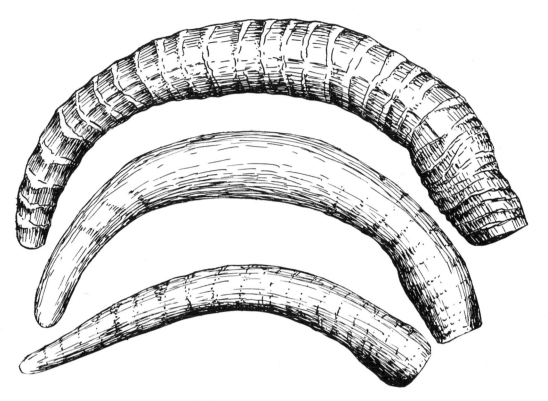

Sickles of Bighorn sheep horn

Deer mandible sickle

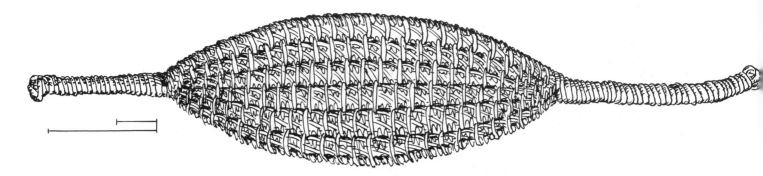

A sling pocket of woven cordage. Such slings may also have been worn as fillets or headbands.

withes, split twigs, rushes and animal fur or hair. The specimens recovered are from dry caves or under very special preservative circumstances such as the 75 or more pairs of woven fiber sandals buried under volcanic pumice in Fort Rock Cave, Oregon. These sandals have a C-14 date of 10,000 years, while twined basketry from Danger Cave, Nevada, dates at about the same level. At the moment these are the oldest known textiles in the world.

Jesse D. Jennings, the excavator of Danger Cave, writing of the basketry, said, "These pieces, along with the Oregon sandals, the twining from Leonard Rockshelter (Nevada) and the twined specimens apparently found on level 4 of Fishbone Cave (Nevada)—all older than 7000 B.C.—permit a suggestion that simple basketry and probably other weaving techniques (e.g. the Fishbone Cave matting) were widely practiced in North America before textile work was known in the Eurasiatic Neolithic." Jennings even goes so far as to speculate that "American weaving is antecedent to Old World textile work" and was possibly introduced into Eurasia from America.

The dry caves of the Great Basin and Oregon have yielded a profusion of evidence of Amerind competence in textiles and basketry. Lovelock Cave produced rodent skin textiles, cordage of several sizes, netting, twined and coiled basketry, and tule matting. The cordage was made of sagebrush, grass, tule, and hemp. The Wendover Caves of Nevada (including Danger, Juke Box and Raven) provided 14 different basketry techniques, 6 of them twining, 8 of them variations of coiling; rabbit and bird skin robes were made, not as early as the textiles and basketry according to the evidence, but in respectably early times. In one reconstructable instance a robe had been crafted of long thin strips of skin wrapped around a cord made of vegetal fibers.

Somewhat farther to the east the bluff shelters of the Ozarks, in Oklahoma have produced fragments of coiled and twined basketry and fur robes, but the East generally is devoid of such remains. The most noted of the deep cave sites, Russell Cave and the Stanfield-Worley Rockshelter in Alabama, Graham Cave in Missouri and Modock Rockshelter in Illinois, are without evidence of basketry or textiles, though in the Sheep Rock Shelter of Pennsylvania the impression of basketry has been found in hardened mud. Other similar instances of basketry and textile impressions are on record.

Fragments of woven cloth and other evidences preserved by metallic salts of copper and silver and found in Hopewell graves show the Hopewellians to have been clothed usually in a fabric that has been variously ascribed to vegetal fibers and "wool." Since wool is made of the

Twined basket

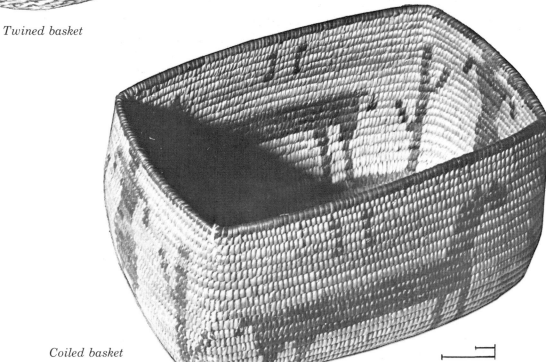

Coiled basket

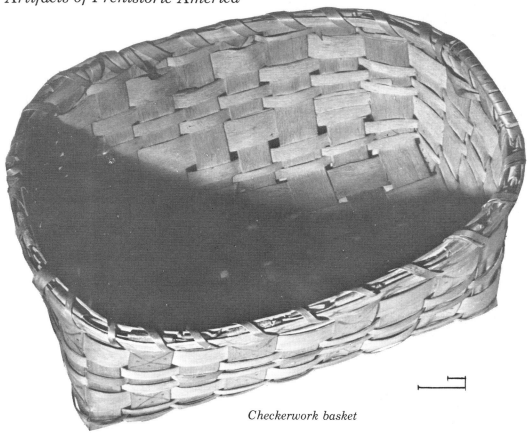

Checkerwork basket

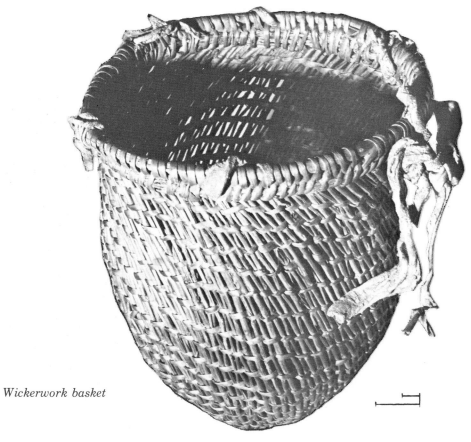

Wickerwork basket

Water bottle; the coiled basket work was impregnated with resins to make it waterproof.

Fine twining

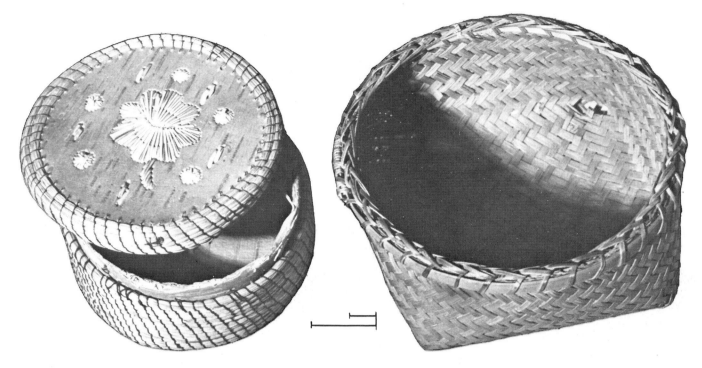

Imbricated (overlapping) twining   *Twillwork*

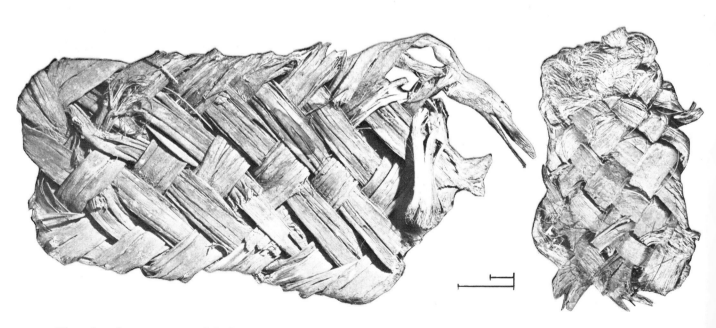

The soles of two woven sandals from Tularosa Cave, New Mexico. A cache of similar sandals was found in Fort Rock Cave, Oregon, and C-14 dated at about 11,000 years ago.

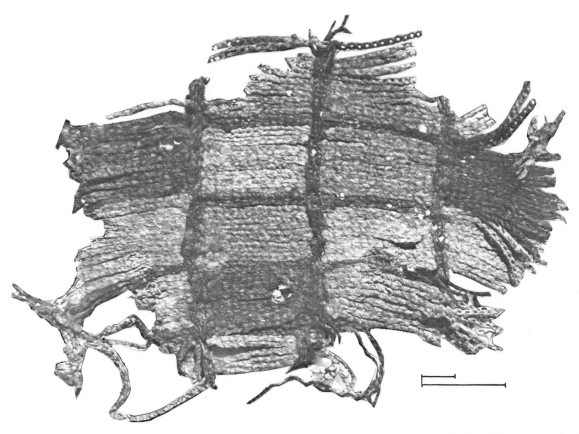

Woven textile fabric from Spiro Mound, Oklahoma. The squares are in four colors—black, red, brown, and yellow.

hair of sheep and no archaeological Amerinds raised sheep, a European import, the hair must have been rabbit fur or the fur of some other animal. The cloth was dyed in batik designs and the skirts of Hopewellian women must have resembled very closely the sarongs of South Sea Island belles. The men wore breech clouts of the same cloth. These details of clothing are quite clear in small realistic statuettes of Hopewell people found in Illinois, the only realistic prehistoric Amerind art found in the United States depicting human beings.

In addition to dry cave contexts and to graves where metallic salts preserve textiles and basketry, the impressions of fabrics, more often basketry, are found in the clay of living floors that had been mud at the time the fabrics or baskets were set there.

chapter 8

Artifacts of Metal

THE AMERINDS OF the prehistoric cultures of the North American continent north of Mexico never learned the secrets of metallurgy. The one metal available to them without metallurgy was native copper which was found in nuggets both on the surface, and later in easily mined veins, in Michigan and Wisconsin. The succession of steps in learning metallurgy is usually: hammering, annealing, melting the native metal, smelting ores, casting and, finally, alloying into bronze. Amerind workmen never got past the hammering and annealing stages, the copper available in most places being about 99 percent pure. There never could have been a Bronze Age in North America, however, because of the absence of tin. Nevertheless the workmanship of the products turned out was of high order.

The Michigan-Wisconsin region was not the only place yielding good copper. Seams and outcrops in Alabama, Georgia, Tennessee, North Carolina, Virginia and Arizona were exploited. In some of these locales a crude kind of smelting to free the copper from the rock matrix was practiced, but it was not metallurgic smelting.

The earliest manufacture of artifacts of copper is documented at the Oconto site in Wisconsin where charcoal from a cremation grave of the so-called "Old Copper" complex tested at 7510 years. From this center the metal, and some of the characteristic artifacts, was traded over the following millenia to the east, west, south and north. Trade routes and perhaps extensions of the Old Copper culture followed both north and south of the Great

Lakes into New York and the Northeast. Old Copper artifacts are found as far west as Nebraska. While only a few copper artifacts are found in the Poverty Point culture of 4000 years ago, the Hopewellians used copper extensively, and thereafter it is common in cultures of the Southeast, but derived from local sources. Some students believe that the Eskimo and Canadian Indian trait of using copper at the white contact time level derived originally from the Old Copper complex. But the copper itself was available from the Coppermine River in Northwest Territories and from the Churchill River, which flows into Hudson Bay.

Copper technology was simple, cold hammering and annealing; that is, softening the metal by heating. Microscopic studies have revealed that the annealing was done in fires that reached as high as 800 degrees C., but well below copper's melting point of 1083 degrees C. The final shaping of the artifact was done by cold hammering. Sheets could be hammered out to one mm thick.

Other metals, meteoric iron, silver and some gold, are found on Middle Woodland Hopewell and later Hopewellian-influenced sites. These occurrences are not evidence of metallurgy or even an interest in metal as such, but only in these exotic materials as

Copper celt and three spear points

Copper axe and ear spool from a Hopewell grave

curiosities or medicine objects. The Hopewells traded as far as the Great Basin and Mexico for obsidian, and the Gulf Coast and perhaps Florida for whelk shell and shark teeth.

Old Copper inventories of copper tools include: awls, chisels, axes, gouges, adzes or spuds, knives, projectile points, crescentic blades, gorges, gaffs, fishhooks, bracelets, rings, clasps and spirally-wound coils. Strangely enough, the Old Copper people made a full line of chipped and polished stone tools, projectile points, knives, bannerstones, and axes. They also polished hematite into geometric forms and probably galena, the lead ore, as well.

The Hopewellians, while they made some implements of copper, such as adzes and axes, directed their efforts in copper working toward ceremonial or ornamental productions: pan-pipes, breastplates, ear spools, cutouts of hands and other designs, bracelets, beads, hair rings and hair pipes, and gorgets.

It has already been mentioned that use was made of metallic ores—galena, which is lead ore, and hematite, an iron ore—but these were not worked even with the simple metallurgy

Probably a copper chisel (bottom) and spear point, Old Copper culture

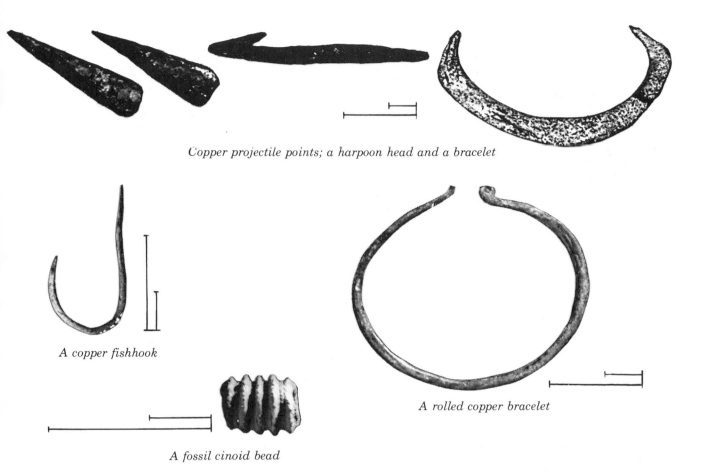

Copper projectile points; a harpoon head and a bracelet

A copper fishhook

A fossil cinoid bead

A rolled copper bracelet

of copper. They were polished as stones, as though they were slate or greenstone, into cones, cubes, hemispheres and cabochons, suggesting charmstone or fetish intent. One other mineral should be added to the list. Sheet mica was favored by some Middle and Late Woodland people, of the Hopewell and Mississippian cultures for cut designs, hands, birds, and cult symbols. But mica, too, was not involved in the transformation we think of as metallurgy. It was no more than a special kind of material fancied for its unique properties, and susceptibility to a simple workmanship.

Two copper adzes

Polished galena hemisphere

A set of handled copper knives

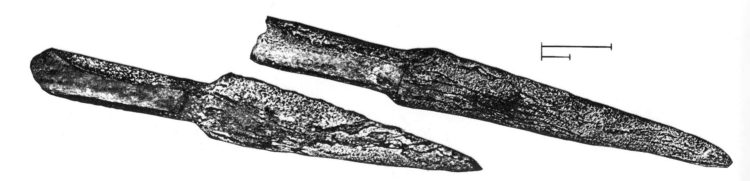

Copper lance or spear heads

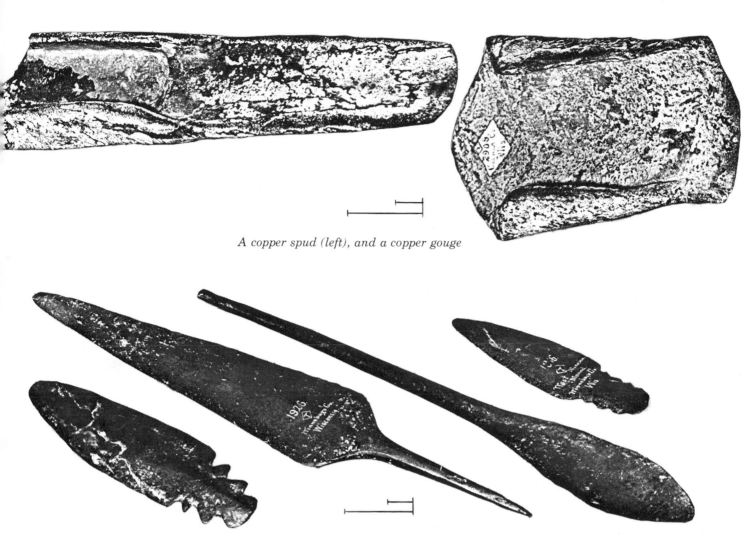

A copper spud (left), and a copper gouge

Two rattail tanged lance heads of copper and two saw-toothed tanged projectile points

A copper awl, upper left; a gouge, lower right; and two chisels.

Copper axe

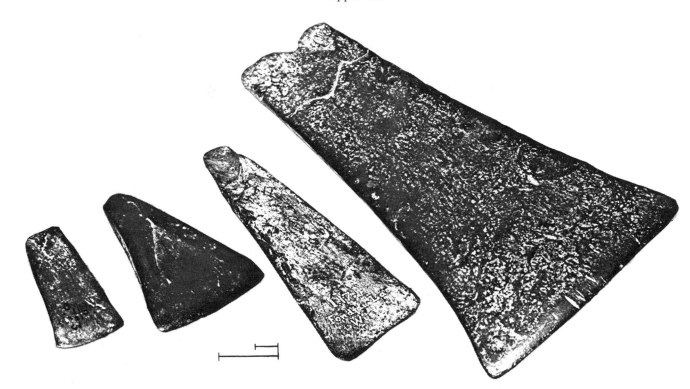

Copper axes of various sizes

Two copper punches or awls

chapter 9

Ceramics

IN THE TECHNOLOGICAL class of ceramics are included all the objects of fired clay: pottery, pipes, figurines, the clay balls known as "Poverty Point objects," and certain other miscellaneous items. A trait of making sun-dried clay objects is found throughout the later prehistory of the Southwest, where caliche, clay mixed with natural salts which bind the clay together into adobe-like adhesion, has been discovered. While it is possible that these dried clay objects preceded pottery and true ceramics, the archaeology does not support an evolution in America of a sun-drying stage of clay modelling as the parental technology for ceramics. The earliest clay pottery known in America is truly ceramic and the most primitive pottery, which is not the earliest, does not appear to evolve out of sun-drying vessel or other forms.

Of the ceramic classes pottery provides the most widespread, abundant and useful evidence for the archaeologist though its manufacture is documented in prehistory in most areas only for three to four thousand years. One broken three-gallon cooking pot can spread enough sherds or fragments across a site to give the archaeologist the impression that he is dealing with an intensive or long-term occupation. In some phases of culture potsherds will far outnumber lithic items and debris, though such a ratio is very rare in the United States. Still, sites producing from 25,000 to 100,000 sherds, enough to put the archaeologist counting potsherds instead of sheep, to a month of nights of fitful slumber.

Pot sherds shaped into gaming discs

In the matter of numbers the Poverty Point objects are next on the list. They run to the millions, but their manufacture is restricted to specific environments and to a relatively brief span of use.

The manufacture of clay pipes begins almost as early as the manufacture of stone pipes and the evolution in form follows that of stone pipes, from the early straight tube to the familiar elbow type, the type adopted by Europeans when they took up smoking. They are commoner in most areas, than the ceramic class of figurines.

Figurines of clay, baked and unbaked, are very rare in the Northeast, but occur in the Middle Woodland and Late Woodland cultures of the Southeast and the Mississippi Valley, and in the A.D. period cultures of the Southwest. The figurines of the Great Basin are likely to be of twigs, but those of California and the Northwest are usually of stone.

In one area of California, however, the flood plains of the lower Sacremento and San Joaquin Rivers, many forms elsewhere made of stone are done in baked clay, ear plugs, labrets, bolas, charmstones and even net sinkers and cupstones. This is one of the three areas in the United States where Poverty Point-like objects are also found.

POVERTY POINT OBJECTS

The Lower Mississippi Valley is, for the most part, of alluvial clay, devoid of the river pebbles that characterize the shores of most freshwater streams. About 4000 years ago the people of the Poverty Point culture found solution to this dearth of the material commonly used for hearths and roasting pits. They began to make fist-sized "balls" of clay as a substitute for pebbles. Probably these balls were not fired originally as ceramics but they soon became ceramic, through repeated use in cooking fires. Ceramic pottery roughly contemporary with these fired balls was rare and tempered with vegetal fiber, not at all like the balls, which were untempered clay except for the sand that naturally occurred in the clay used.

These objects were made between cupped hands like snowballs, but they are never spheres that would roll like a ball. In general shape they are cylindrical or biconical, spheroid, melon-shaped or, infrequently, cuboid. Using attributes of shape, exterior impressions, and occasionally decoration, it has been possible to separate out over a hundred different "types," surprising in so utilitarian and commonly manufactured an item. That they were made by hand of plastic mud no doubt accounts for a certain play of fancy in their shaping, but that the same types appear on sites quite distant from each other remains to be explained.

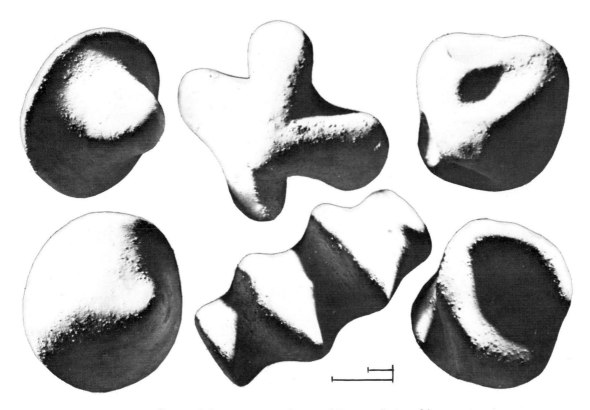

Some of the commoner forms of Poverty Point objects

The clay objects from the Sacramento River area of California are roughly contemporary with the Poverty Point culture half a continent away and the reason for their manufacture and use may be the same, a lack of stone and an ubiquity of clay. It is generally believed that some of the California specimens were, like the Poverty Point objects, substitute cooking stones. But the fact that some of them were decorated with techniques used on pottery (though no pottery was ever made in this area) suggests other unknown uses. In this area, as mentioned above, many items elsewhere made of stone were duplicated in baked clay.

The third region where baked clay "balls" are found is on the Atlantic side of the continent, along the Georgia coast. The best guess is that these would have been used as a substitute for stone "boilers" even though a certain amount of primitive, fiber-tempered pottery appears to be contemporary with them. The Georgia coast and coastal islands' "balls" are fiber-tempered and not as numerous or as various in style as the Poverty Point collection. They are associated with "structures" of circles made of banks of shell and fall into the same time period, generally, as the Poverty Point and California manifestations.

TETRAHEDRONS

Rather like the Poverty Point objects found on Poverty Point sites but different in shape, and therefore almost certainly different in function, is the class of baked clay objects called tetrahedrons from their rough pyramidical form. The best guess is that these were supports for clay vessels sitting in a fire for heating the contents. Out of the thousands found, fewer than ten are complete so that it has not been possible to discover whether the collection is divisible into types. If they are vessel supports they must be later than most Poverty Point objects, or are at least late in the long Poverty Point culture tenure of, perhaps, 800 years. They must be adaptations of the Poverty Point idea of substitution of baked clay for stone. Most of the pottery vessels used for cooking had conoidal bottoms, so that they had to be supported from the side in order to remain vertical. Where stone was available pebbles were used as supports. Early on, Amerinds discovered that conoidal-based vessels set in a nest of hot coals heated more quickly than flat-bottomed pots.

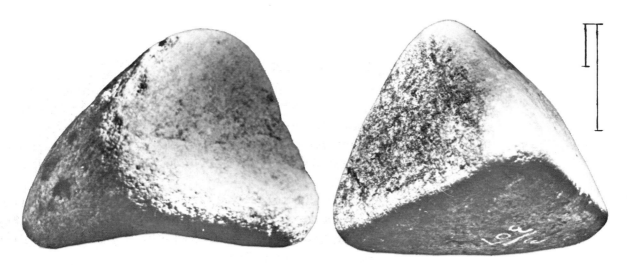

Tetrahedrons or pot supports. These are of stone, but they are the prototypes imitated in ceramic.

PIPES

Baked clay was used as a material for pipes almost as soon as stone. It may have been used in some areas even before the introduction of ceramic pottery. The earliest pipe forms, straight tubes and cigar-shaped tubes were made in both stone and baked clay and there are even some rare apparent instances of clay platform pipes, though these are probably not classic Hopewellian. The trend in pipe shape from straight tube to the bent, with bowl and stem at obtuse or right angles to each other, probably marks the change in use of the pipe from a shaman's implement to a smoking device. The straight tubes were probably exhaled through, to make medicine fumes or smoke. But when the bowl and stem began to be angled in relation to each other the draft was reversed to inhalation. Pipes grow more numerous throughout the Late Woodland and it is obvious that smoking began to be indulged in as a personal habit, though ceremonial pipes, "calumets" or medicine pipes, continue in vogue. The personal smoking pipes were made of clay and appear in many styles of shape and decoration including effigies. The skulls of Indians have been recovered with a worn arch in the teeth typical of habitual smoking of the abrasive clay stemmed ceramic pipes.

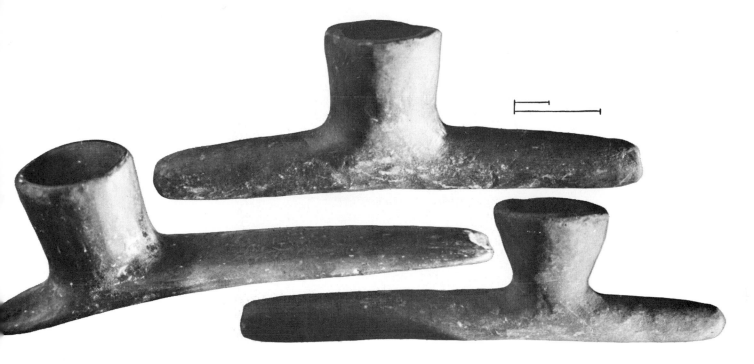

Ceramic platform pipe, center. Below, two platform-like ceramic pipes with round stems.

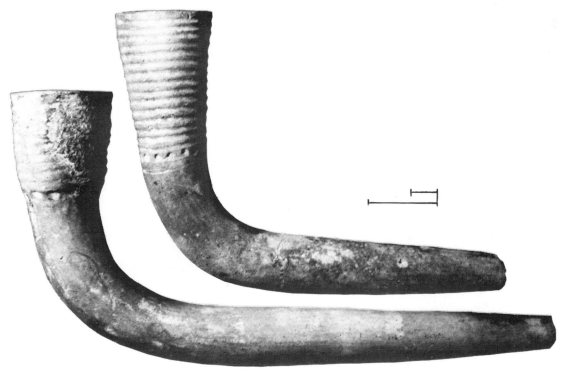

Late prehistoric ceramic pipes

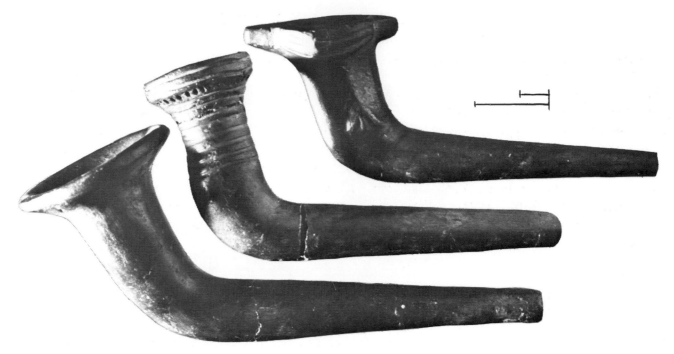

Iroquoisian "trumpet" style pipes

FIGURINES

Figurines are a class of singular representations of the human figure or face, not attached to or a part of pipes, pots or other artifacts. They range from the realistic to the most rudimentary stylistic, more often the latter, hardly more than sausages of baked clay with a minimum of indicated features. Whether they were cult objects, anthropomorphic images of mythic personages or supernal powers, or reminders of the dead is not known.

Figurine head from a Mississippian site

MISCELLANEOUS OBJECTS

As mentioned concerning "Poverty Point objects," in the Sacramento River area an industry developed in the manufacture of objects of baked clay that were commonly made elsewhere of stone, apparently because of the scarcity of stone within their habitation territory. Neither the Poverty Point people nor the Georgia coast people resorted to such substitution, preferring to import stone, trade for it or send parties out to get it. The only substitution was for hearth and roasting pit stones, used in such quantities that transportation was impractical. But the Hopewellian artisans, in exuberant display of their versatility, reproduced common items such as ear spools, in baked clay, covering them with copper sheeting and otherwise elaborating them. On the assumption that even at this late date not all kinds of artifacts have been found, and not all traditions have been described, the archaeologist may expect to find baked clay forms duplicating most classes of artifacts in use during the ceramic period.

POTTERY

It appears that the manufacture of ceramic pottery had two beginnings in the New World: invention in possibly two different places, and by transplant from, of all unlikely places, the Island of Kyushu, Japan.

The archaeological evidence places a center of the manufacture of a vegetal fiber (mostly grass) tempered pottery at Puerto Hormiga, on the north coast of Colombia slightly in excess of 5100 C-14 years ago; this is the earliest date on ceramic pottery in either America. Although it is decorated, the Puerto Hormiga pottery is so rudimentary that it would seem to be near the invention stage. An even more rudimentary fiber-tempered pottery, undecorated, has been found at several sites along the southern Georgia and Florida Atlantic coast; it dates at about 4000 C-14 years ago. No trail of evidence connects the Colombian pottery with the Georgia-Florida pottery overland and the plausible suggestion has been made that the fiber-tempering manufacturing process may have been carried by boat across the Gulf of Mexico. While Puerto Hormiga is by no means the nearest port from which pottery makers might have embarked to make a landfall along the Florida-Georgia coast, the close clustering for initial dates for fiber-tempered pottery there is consistent with an influx of colonists. On the other hand, the Georgia-Florida pottery is undecorated and the Colombian pottery, of an age of 4000 C-14 years ago, was decorated, leaving a clear possibility that the former at pottery's most primitive stage, was an independent invention.

For the second center of 5000-year-old pottery, on the Pacific coast of Ecuador near the village of Valdivia, there is no better explanation than that advanced by the excavators of the Valdivia culture, that a boatload of castaway fishermen of the Japanese Jomon period had landed there and introduced the local shore-dwelling population to the techniques and art of ceramics. Although the earliest Valdivia pottery is rather inexpertly made, the decorations and surface treatments are advanced, running almost the full gamut of practices found in later pottery in both South and North America: incising, punctation, rocker stamping, scraping, grooving, applique, polishing, and slipping. The Valdivia excavators, Betty J. Meggers and Clifford Evans of the Smithsonian Institution, point out that the

Fiber-tempered sherds. Note the stringy lines in the center sherd; these are casts of the grassy fiber used as temper.

"variety of decorative techniques and vessel shapes seems incongruous in the oldest pottery in the New World." But this variousness would not be surprising had the Valdivia pottery been introduced from a full-blown pottery tradition, like the Jomon, which the decorative techniques and vessel shapes remarkably resemble. Pottery manufacture began in Japan between 11,000 and 10,000 years ago.

It is true that the Puerto Hormiga pottery is decorated, though the decorations are not those of Valdivia, but the principal differences are that the Valdivia pottery is sand-tempered and made by coiling, while the Puerto Hormiga pottery is fiber-tempered and hand-modelled.

Valdivia and Colombian pottery may, or may not, account for all subsequent pottery traditions in South and Meso-America; they certainly account for many of the main cur-

Curvilinear design bowl from the Southeast

rents. In North America the plain fiber-tempered ware of Georgia-Florida prevailed for about 500 years, spreading across the Southeast and appearing in the Poverty Point culture at about 3600 C-14 years ago. Decoration begins to appear about 3500 C-14 years ago and fiber-tempered ware continued to be made until about 3000 C-14 years ago. What pushed it into obsolescence was the pottery known as the Woodland tradition.

Woodland pottery made its entrance on the archaeological scene about 3000 years ago, or about 1000 B.C. That entrance seems to have been simultaneous over the northeast quadrant of the present United States, northward of an east-west line from Virginia to the Mississippi Valley. It is a coil made pottery, grit-tempered and surface-textured by paddling the surface with a cord-wrapped stick or spatulate beater. Later in the tradition other surface treatments were used, fabric-marking, net-marking and scraping and smoothing over the cord marking. In the beginning cord-marking was not a decorative feature; later, in some areas, the edge of the cord-wrapped paddle or a cord-wrapped wand or stick was used to create decorative motifs.

Woodland pottery surface treatments: 1. Smoothed-over cordmarking. 2. Cordmarking; 3. The frayed end of a twig was used to produce this effect. 4. This surface was daubed with a wad of netting. 5. A smooth surface that may have been produced by rubbing with a pebble. 6. A net-impressed surface showing the net knots in stretched-out order; 7, 8 and 9 are textile-impressed sherds.

Various kinds of cord-marking by malleating with a cord-wrapped flat paddle. The first and third (below) are interior cord-marked.

THE WOODLAND TRADITION

The assumption was, when Woodland pottery was first defined as a tradition, that it had its origin in Asia and had arrived here from the Siberian-Alaskan port of entry. Forty years of archaeology have turned up no evidence of such an origin. One suggestion, that it was implanted in America by castaways from northern Europe, as the Kyushu fishermen implanted the Valdivia pottery, has met with little favor among archaeologists. At the moment its appearance in America remains unexplained. The earliest Woodland pottery, called Vinette I in the Northeast and Half-moon Cord-marked and Fayette Thick in the Ohio Valley, suggests anything but the transplanting of a going tradition. The vessels are small, thick-walled, conoidal-based, tempered with heavy grit and not well-fired. The one feature that bespeaks the importation is the coil-winding method of manufacture, and that is no more than the adoption of one simple idea. It is as though someone had witnessed the manufacture of coiled pottery and remembered the building up of the vessel by laying coils or fillets of clay one on top of the other and bonding them together by malleation with a cord-wrapped paddle. While his observation was accurate, his experience was slight, and the result was imitation, with all the shortcomings.

It has already been stated that fiber-tempered pottery spread from its apparent center

A pottery stamp from Mexico with an Aztecan design. It is made of clay.

An intaglio design in a Mississippian vessel. The raised areas are red, the intaglio design is the gray of the clay.

on the Georgia-Florida coast to the southern Mississippi Valley. But it did not really take hold there and the manufacture of ceramic pottery did not become a flourishing trait until the introduction, from somewhere in Mexico of what is generally called clay-tempered ware. Technically, the tempering material is called grog, and consists of the pieces of crushed sherds of broken pots. There is some controversy about whether this tempering is always sherd fragments or may not be particles of dried clay included in the wet clay when it was being worked. It is a specialist's argument. While some sand is included in the paste from which the vessels are made, probably as a result of the kind of clay chosen, the intention of the potter was clearly to use hard clay particles as an aplastic. The tradition begins with the Tchefuncte pottery of a Louisiana shellfish using people at about the time that Woodland pottery began to be made, about 3000 C-14 years ago. It differs from Woodland pottery in that it was smooth-surfaced from the use of the pottery trowel rather than the cord or textile-covered paddle. Continuing influences from Mexico or Meso-America effected changes in decoration and vessel shape but the ware itself threads the whole of ceramic prehistory in the Mississippi Valley.

There are areas of overlap of Woodland, mainly Hopewellian, and Mississippian pot-

Close-up of the intaglio design. It appears to be an elaboration of the engraving technique.

tery, especially in the Southeast, and the ceramics of the prairies and to some extent of the plains is a mixture of the two.

East of the Appalachians there is an overlap of Woodland and southern fiber-tempered ceramics. The manufacture of steatite vessels was more or less contemporary with the manufacture of fiber-tempered pottery, possibly because the fiber-tempered ware was not entirely satisfactory and steatite was better for certain uses. Shortly before the appearance of Woodland pottery in the east, by the dates we now have, the residents of Virginia, Maryland and the southern Delaware and Susquehanna Valleys began to make a ware called Marcy Creek, which imitates steatite vessels in shape, being flat-bottomed and straight-sided, and is mineral-tempered. But the mineral is steatite. The Marcy Creek ware was short-lived, overwhelmed by the robust Woodland tradition.

Most readers, when they advert to the subject of native pottery, think of the painted wares of the Southwest, whence has come so much of the native pottery to be seen in museums and where native pottery manufacture continues today. They may be surprised, therefore, to learn that pottery manufacture came late to the Southwest, about 100 B.C. in the Mogollon area of southern New Mexico and Arizona, and some centuries later in the Anasazi (Basketmaker-Pueblo) region to the north, in the Four Corners area of New Mexico, Arizona, Colorado, and Utah. The first Southwestern pottery was plain, with the exception of one red-slipped type, San Francisco Red, and most vessels were polished with a pebble. The exact ancestry has not been determined but there is no question of its derivation from somewhere to the Mexican south. It is certainly neither primitive nor invented. Since pottery never reached California, except very late, at the extreme southern desert tip, nor the Northwest, the Southwest is the last region within the present United States where the trait became aboriginally established.

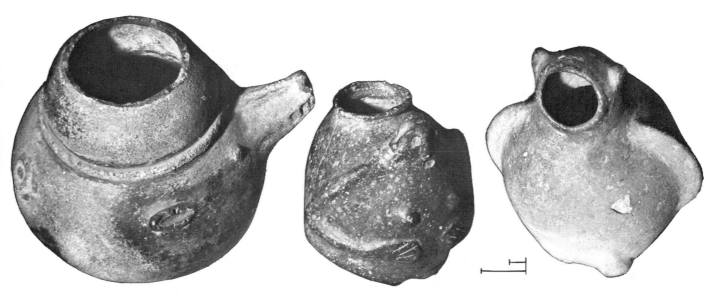

Mississippian effigy vessels. At left, a fox or wolf; center, the "hunchback woman," a recurring motif; at right, an owl, possibly a horned owl.

A pottery stamp, left, and a pottery trowel, both of stone.

WARES AND TYPES

With so long and varied and puzzling a history it is hardly to be wondered at that this is the archaeologist's biggest headache. As one authority put it "Pottery types are almost as numerous as trees in the forests of eastern North America." There seems to be no perfect taxonomy of pottery and the only way to handle the millions of sherds so as to be able to

Thumbnail impressions as decoration on an incised design

abstract any anthropological information from them is by computer, which is not totally satisfactory either. The computer's skills are mathematical, not anthropological. By and large the archaeologist has to work with a loose but manageable classification of wares and types. The ware is the broader classification and may include a group of types or several series of types. The type is determined by its modes which are, in turn, concurrences of features. The feature is "the smallest recognizable single element that is observable in the pottery under study." Fiber-tempering is a feature; punctuation with a fingernail is a feature; notched lip is a feature. If a feature is "demonstrated to have cultural and historical significance, it is considered a mode." Or a mode can consist of a combination of features that consistently appear together. Dentate stamping in zones or plats is a combination of features constituting a mode.

The following is a standard description of a ware, Weaver Ware, found on Hopewell sites in Illinois:

Tempering: crushed rocks; particles abundant and fine.

Texture: compact.

Hardness: around 3.0 (Mohs' Hardness Scale)

Color: reddish tan, with some grays and blacks; cores rarely different.

Surface finish: plain surface, with some very hard finish looking like polished surface cord marking of tightly twisted cord on vertical parallel lines.

Decoration: rims notched or stamped with cord-wrapped stick, paddle edge or plain stamp; lips sometimes scalloped; embossed nodes present.

Form: conoidal or globular jars with vertical rims.

Dimensions: diameters up to 18 inches; walls 6 to 10mm thick.

A type description, that of the clay-tempered Tchefuncte Plain, is as follows:

Method of manufacture: coiled, sherds break readily along coil lines.

Tempering: angular pieces of clay, with some sand; occasionally scraps of carbonized vegetal matter.

Texture: paste is very fine but poorly wedged resulting in lamination and contortion during firing.

Hardness: about 2.0 on Mohs' Scale; that is, very soft and with little tensile strength.

Color: reddish buff to dark gray, with black, carbonized core.

Surface finish: surface has been floated; that is, rubbed while paste was wet to bring fine clay particles to surface resulting in soft, chalky finish which flakes off readily.

Form:

Rim: straight or slightly curved, in or out. On some vessels the rim is turned over or a strap of clay is added and rounded into the rim.

Lip: usually rounded, sometimes casually notched.

Body: deep pot, with straight sides at rim, slight bulging in middle, lower walls converging to a flattened base supported by four legs. In some examples walls outflare at rim.

Base: supports are teat-shaped or wedge-leg, rarely annular or ring shaped.

Range: Louisiana, during the Tchefuncte period.

Breaks in coil-wound pottery. The bottom two sherds show the negative or indented joint of the coil. The top three show the rounded or positive joint.

ATTRIBUTES AND MODES

The foregoing ware and type descriptions have introduced the main headings under which attributes are listed for the purpose of recognizing related groupings. Attributes are comparatively limited; the number of ways in which they can be combined run to the thousands. Only the closest students will know all the types and varieties of the areas where they work for years. A few specialists know the ceramics of a region; but they have to keep at it. New types keep turning up almost weekly and recently a student of Delaware Valley prehistory has stumbled on the interesting fact that several sherds he came upon in a dig would have been typed as coming from different varieties of ceramics of different time periods if they had not all fit together very snugly. The way sherds should be examined is, roughly, as follows:

Method of manufacture

The clay for well-made aboriginal pottery was not only carefully selected but carefully prepared by pounding with a hammerstone until it was flour soft, with all stones and pebbles removed. That the clay was so thoroughly prepared from the beginning is questionable, though it is not always possible to separate immanent inclusions in the clay from the tempering.

Tempering is added as the clay is wet down and worked into the consistency of putty. Nearly everything that could possibly serve that purpose has been used at one time or another in one place or another; grass, clay, wood fibers, leaves, sand, crushed grit, grog and lumps of clay, even feathers. But the principal tempering or aplastic materials were, as previously noted, vegetal fiber (which had a comparatively limited area of use), clay, (either grog or fragments of broken pots, or intentionally or carelessly included lumps of unfired clay), volcanic ash, sand and crushed rock or grit. The microscopic analysis of clay and tempering materials has been a very fertile field of cultural data. The function of temper is to prevent excessive shrinking of the dried clay. Certain clays, the residual clays (as contrasted with sedimentary clays deposited by water action) are grainy and do not require tempering, and some sedimentary clays are so fine that they shrink very little. In the Woodland pottery region, however, there is a chronological succession in tempering, heavy grit being the temper of the earliest pottery. The tempering becomes successively finer, and the pottery thinner and harder and less porous, over time. In some areas the available clay required no tempering and no aplastic was ever part of the tradition. Where vegetal fiber was used it was mostly destroyed in firing, leaving holes or cells, so that this kind of pottery was once called cell-tempered.

The three methods of building a vessel are: molding, coiling, and modelling. Molding is known from only two areas, in Mexico and Peru, and these areas are not large; it is the formation of a pot within or over a hard mold. Though the use of baskets as molds has sometimes been suggested, it is not a probable practice, since the basket would have to be destroyed to free the pot for firing or in firing.

Modelling is the direct shaping of a vessel by hand from a lump of clay. The work is done by holding an anvil stone inside the vessel being shaped and beating the clay over it with a wooden mallet or paddle.

Coiling is the build up of vessel walls by laying rings or coils of clay on top of each other and bonding them by the paddle and anvil method. Coil-wound vessels often break along coil junctions, revealing the method to the archaeologist. But the two methods of modelling and coil-winding are sometimes used on the same vessel, the bottom being formed by modelling and the upper part by coiling.

In Woodland pottery the paddle used was wrapped with cord, the purpose being, apparently, to bond the coils more firmly by the mixing effect of rough impact surface of the paddle. There is no doubt that this cord-marking was not an intentional decorative treatment but a step in the manufacturing process. In the very earliest Woodland pottery, the type called Vinette I for instance, there is a concomitant cord-marking on the interior of the vessel, the cording running at approximately right angles to the trend of those on the surface. In later pottery this interior cord-marking is smoothed over or scraped over, by hand, by smooth pebbles, with shell or with a handful of leaves or grass. Such smoothing or scraping is also found on the exterior surface, usually after pots have begun to be decorated by stamping and incising.

The paddle was, in many instances, covered with some kind of textile, a swatch of woven cord or netting. There is a tradition of pottery along the Mid-Atlantic seaboard of treating the surface and sometimes the interior, with a wad of netting held in the hand, which was the paddle. Experiments have shown that the cord-marking on some vessels must have been

Various designs made by impression with a round cord-wrapped stick. In No. 6 the cord impressions have been smoothed over and almost obliterated. No. 8 is an example of the rare pseudo-scallop shell marking; the design seems to have been made by the edge of a scallop shell, but the line of indentations is straight, not curved like a scallop shell.

done by suspending the vessel in a net-like bag and then malleating it, probably with a pebble.

It seems clear in all Woodland pottery that surface marking, whether left without further treatment or smoothed over, was a tenaciously believed-in principle of construction.

From the beginning the fiber-tempered ware of the Southeast and the clay-tempered ware of the mid-South and the Mississippi Valley were smooth-surfaced. Ceramicists note that pottery evolution in these areas produced an earlier emphasis on decoration and a much wider variety of vessel shapes than in the Woodland area. Woodland potters never did make anything as complex in shape as the tetrapodal, or four-footed, vessel described above for the initial Tchefuncte ware and were never capable of (that is, their ceramic tradition never fitted them for) the manufacture of the often elegant effigy pottery of later stages of Mississippian and Missippian-influenced traditions. In short, the Mississippian potters early learned plastic design, and adopted methods of manufacture suited to it. Only in pipe design does the Northeast tradition produce ceramic molding of other than geometric shapes. The faces on Northeast pots are mere child's punched eyes-nose-mouth sketches, whereas the Missippian and later southern potters executed realistic faces and a whole range of animal forms and stylized designs in three dimensions.

The Missippian potters used the pottery trowel, a smooth-faced, flat implement of baked clay or stone, against an interior anvil with what appears to have been a combination of malleation and smoothing. The bottom half or so of pots was hand-modelled, with the rest built up by non-coil increments which made it possible to hand-model effigy rims and designed spouts, etc.

The potters of the Southwest took a somewhat different route. The vessels are smooth-finished, sometimes slipped and polished, with the intention of obtaining color and color contrast. Much of this pottery obtains its effect from painting designs on a pleasingly contrasting color on the basic color of the fired clay, thus ware names such as red-on-buff or

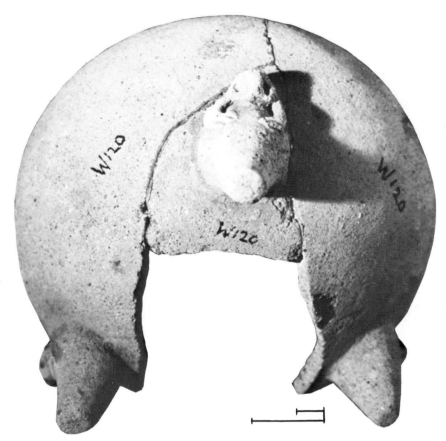

A lizard figure on the leg of a Mississippian pot

black-on-white. One ware is exceptional to the foregoing, the corrugated utility ware made widely throughout the Southwest. This is a coil-wound pottery in which the successive layers have coils which have been pushed down so that they overlap the one below on the outside. This overlap is not smoothed over or scraped away and remains as a series of fringes which are sometimes finger-pinched or notched, sometimes not. Coiling, modelling and a combination of the two gave Southwestern potters considerable versatility in designing vessel shapes.

Vessel Form

The vessel forms of Woodland can almost be reduced to one form with varying dimensions, a large or small bag-shaped cooking pot. The bases are conoidal or rounded for placing in the fire, not over it, and the body swells to its maximum diameter at about the middle of the height, either maintaining this diameter to the lip or constricting into a vasiform. A graceful neck was not achieved until rather late and soon after, about A.D. 1100 a collar was added that, as it grew in depth and was decorated with castellations or apexes on the rim, destroyed any artistic merit the pottery may have achieved. Only the artistically gifted Hopewellians ever broke away from the pot shape and then only in ceremonial ware.

Southeastern pottery, while it was under Woodland influence, was in the typical Woodland shapes but was much imaginative in its decoration. About A.D. 900 it came under

Two Mississippian vessel forms

Mississippian vessel form

Engraving on a Mississippian pot

Southwestern painted pottery

Southwestern pottery, reverse design

Cord-on-cord impressed pottery. A cord-wrapped stick was used to provide a decorative design on a background of cord-wrapped paddle malleated surface.

Southwestern corrugated pottery. Third piece in from left (above) is a bottom base.

Southeastern pottery decoration. The third piece from left (top row) is a punctate-decorated sherd. Beside it (right) is a check stamp. The piece below it is a textile design. The others are complicated stamp design.

the liberating influence of Mississippian traditions and all kinds of shapes began to appear, as they did in the Mississippi Valley: water bottles, dippers, urns, pans, dishes, vases, crocks, "beanpots," "cuspidors," bowls. These forms were executed with great versatility, in effigy and other imaginative shapes.

The forms of Southwestern pottery range basically through as wide a variety as Missippian pottery and much the same forms, with some added ones, handled mugs and "pitchers," cups and funnels. The element missing from the Southwest is the figure sculpting, and the artistic fancy.

The rim forms of pottery in all areas are considered attributes. The angle, and there are many, the rim makes with the vessel is often diagnostic, but they are essentially straight, in-turned or flaring, and rounded or squared rim castellations. Rims rising to one or more peaks out of the horizontal are confined to Northeast pottery though, strangely enough, a sherd with a castellation was found in the lowest level at Valdivia. The rims of Mississippian, Southeastern and Southwestern pottery are seldom out of the level. They are horizontal except for handles or effigies though there are some few notched, scalloped, dipped or mildly castellated versions. The ingenious potters of these traditions would not have overlooked such variations; they simply did not seem to be interested in them.

Decoration

The three principal methods of decoration are: impressing or stamping, incising and painting. A fourth method, applique, or the attaching of elements of design to a pot, is not of much importance, which makes it highly diagnostic when it is found, usually on Mississippian wares. a fifth method, engraving, is an adaptation of incising.

Punctation is the simplest form of stamping or impressing. It consists of making one impression at a time, usually in linear order. The points used in punctation were of various

Incised decorative motifs. The second one in at left (below) has a castellated rim.

Bottoms and holes. Nos. 1, 3 and 4 are the bottom bosses or nodes of pots. The holes in Nos. 2, 3, 4 and 5 have been drilled as repair holes.

kinds; fingernails, pointed sticks or bone or antler, hollow reeds or finger ends. While these impressions are usually made on exterior surfaces, punching a blunted instrument—usually a finger—from the inside made a knob on the outside; such a knob is called a node. Nodes were a Hopewellian trait. Punctation is usually used to underline other design elements, though punctates may appear in what seems to be random placement.

Not to be confused with punctates are repair holes drilled through the pot wall to stop cracks from running and widening. The repair hole was plugged with wood, fiber, or leather.

The *dentate stamp* is a toothed linear tool like a comb, that leaves a row of puncture marks. It has been suggested that, in addition to combs, fish backbones were used in dentate stamping. But dentate stamps may have been made of wood, bone or stone. Certain shells, with toothed edges, such as the scallop, have been identified as a dentate stamp and shells are usually the tool used in what is called rocker stamping, in which the stamp is pressed in one direction and then reversed at a slightly different angle, in a frieze effect. It is probably not accurate to call dentate stamping roulette stamping since it is doubtful that aboriginal potters ever used a roulette or toothed wheel. The stamping on some clay pipes may, however, be authentic rouletting, since such pipes are post-European contact.

What casual inspection will often misidentify as dentate stamping turns out to be *cord stamping*, with the edge of a cord-wrapped paddle or a cord-wrapped thin stick. The cords, where they turn the edge, make small regular indentations in a straight line. The use of this decorative technique became very popular in the Northeast, and is general over the Woodland area, though it is less common in the Midwest.

Another dentate stamping look-alike is *stab-and-drag* or drag-and-jab punctation, a technique found more often in southern Woodland pottery than in the Northeast quadrant. The punctating tool remains in contact with the pot surface between holes, making a line of connected dots.

Historically, in the Woodland region, punctation seems the earliest attempt at impressed decoration, followed by dentate stamping and then by corded-edged paddle stamp-

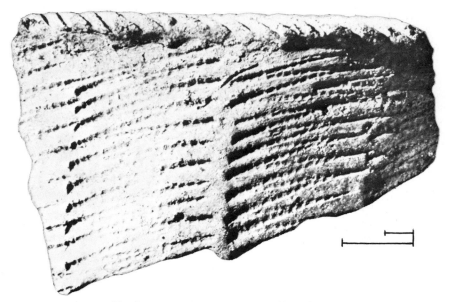

Rocker stamping, using a scallop shell

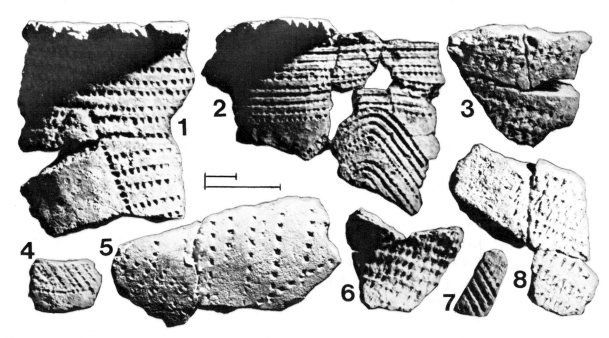

Stamping techniques: In No. 1 a square-toothed stamp was used; it apparently had six teeth, judging by the recurrence of the tooth pattern. In No. 2 two different stamps were used, one with square-teeth and one with round teeth; the two upper arched lines are stab-and-drag. No. 3 is a simple dentate design. No. 4 is a pseudo-dentate design, made by a single-pointed implement applied with a kind of striking rather than punch motion. No. 5 is smoothed-over dentate. No. 6 is a "scratch" pseudo-dentate. No. 7 is actually a punctate rather than a dentate design, made by a single pointed implement; the tip-off is the stab-and-drag middle line. No. 8 is a sort of random dentate, not made by an implement with teeth in line.

A mixture of techniques on the same sherd. At left, a cord-marked rim sherd with incised decoration. Interior of same sherd (right) with shell scraped surface and cord-wrapped stick-impressed decoration on lip.

ing. In the Northeast these are the only stamping techniques. But in the Woodland territory in the South stamping with a paddle carved with the design to be impressed came early into vogue. The earliest "simple stamped" designs are merely lines, in the very beginning probably made with a stick or dowel or paddle edge. But this soon became a real stamp, with a reiterative design in straight lines, then cross-hatched and then "complicated stamp" designs of nested circles and fylfot crosses. A kind of intermediate design between the simple and the complicated stamp is the check stamp, a wafflelike pattern.

In the Northeast the dentate and cord-stamping designs are on the upper part of the vessel, on the neck and rim. Southeastern stamping, however, usually covers the whole vessel.

Whether net and fabric impressing and corn-cob stamping are truly stamping techniques, or are merely variations on Woodland tradition, surface texturing is a question that could be answered only by the potters themselves. In Woodland wares surface texturing is, as applied, a concomitant of the manufacturing process. Left on the vessel, it might be assumed to have a decorative intent. That it was often scraped or smoothed over seems to say that it was not considered attractive for its own sake. On the other hand the elaboration of motifs in Southern pottery paddle stamping bespeaks decorative intent, even while the paddling was a step in the manufacturing process. On the whole, net and fabric impression and the much later corn-cob stamping would appear to be texturing techniques, executed for some real or fancied practical value, rather than prettifying additions.

To sum up, surface impressing by stamping is strongly characteristic of Woodland pottery, wherever found, and wherever found is regarded as diagnostic of Woodland ceramics. The minor amounts of punctating and stamping found in Mississippian pottery beginning at, perhaps, A.D. 800, are carry-overs from Woodland predecessors.

A case could be made for the proposition that *incising*, the creation of linear designs by a pointed stylus of wood, bone, antler or stone, is correlated with plain-surface pottery. The

Interior treatments in Woodland pottery: Nos. 1 and 3 are "channelled," the smoothing implement apparently a stick. No. 2 has been hand-smoothed, with depressions caused by finger tips. Nos. 4, 5 and 6 have been smoothed with a hard-surface implement, either a stone or another pot sherd; the scratch lines in No. 6 show that these smoothers were sometimes jagged. No. 7 has been smoothed with a clam shell. No. 8 is interior cord-marked and No. 9 is smoothed-over cord-marked, apparently with a handful of grass.

first decorative efforts of the makers of the fiber-tempered ware of Georgia-Florida, after 400-500 years of undecorated pots, the types Ticks Island and Orange, were toward decoration by inscribing or incising. The designs were, moreover, curvilinear, "drawing" in the design sense. Incising did not appear until very late in the Northeast and then only as stiff, straight line arrangements of monotonous triangular or geometric zones or plats, with horizontal underlines. Curvilinear incising first appeared in Woodland pottery among the Hopewellians, who created scrollwork patterns, stylized serpent and bird forms and motifs such as concentric circles.

Mississippian potters used incising most freely in the ways described above and in adumbrating the features of effigies and other modelled forms. But then, Mississippi pottery, overall and not in any one place at one time, includes all the elements discussed previously; incising, punctating, stamping in all forms, painting and applique.

Painting is the last of the decorative techniques of native pottery. Color is the key to Southwest pottery, even when that pottery is not painted. Unpainted pottery was usually highly polished to enhance the hue, with grease being wiped on the surface during the polishing process. Vessels which were to be painted were usually slipped; that is, several coats of colored clay in a solution of the consistency of the cream of milk, were applied before painting. The paint was brushed on with fiber brushes in freehand designs, when the painting was direct. In negative painting the background was colored in and the design itself was the color of the clay. In resist painting the area of the design was covered with wax and the whole vessel painted with the wax melting away when the vessel was heated, leaving the design in the background color. Negative and resist painting are difficult to distinguish. All three kinds of painting are found in Mississippian pottery after about A.D. 800, but painting is only one of the several decorative techniques used by Mississippian period potters, whereas it is the main technique in the Southwest.

The first ware to enter the Mogollon territory of the Southwest was a plain, polished red or brown ceramic, with painting of rather crude designs in red on the brown pots a second generation type. It is interesting to note that in all pottery areas the initial pottery was plain ware, except in the Woodland area. Types of plain pottery continued to be made in all areas, including the Woodland, but in the Woodland area the plainess is secondary; that is, the pottery became plain only after smoothing over or scraping over the surface texturing.

Applique has already been described, and there is very little else about it to discuss. It is found mainly in the Mississippian area, where it is obviously related to modelling. But there is one final decorative technique that bears mention. It is *engraving*, which is incising on the surface of the already fired pot. Engraving is found on some Mississippian and Southwest ceramics. Incising and stamping were done, of course, in the soft, prefired surface. Engraving is important as a type attribute, but it was not in widespread use.

Although Mohs' Scale hardness is usually mentioned in ware and type descriptions, *it is not regarded as a significant attribute* because clays are so variable in their reaction to firing. While the accuracy of the firing required by a particular clay can be seen in the color of the core or interior of a sherd if it is different from that of the outside, conclusions about firing are best left to the laboratory ceramicist. No aboriginal pottery was ever fired in a kiln, but temperatures could be reached by the fuel and methods at hand to fire all clays adequately. Which is not to say that glazing was ever attained, so that all native pottery is to a degree porous. In the Southwest and, perhaps elsewhere, interiors were treated with gums or other fillers to prevent leakage, probably not a serious problem as most Amerinds saw it.

Pottery identification does not come easy, because the archaeologist rarely sees pottery except in from a few to a hundred fragments of the original pot. To acquire what archaeologists call "pottery sense" requires the handling of thousands of sherds and years of experience, with a perceptive eye and a kind of intuition, which is nothing more than a

Southwest painted pottery

217

Southwest painted pottery

growing sense of what wares and types look like. All sorts of attributes can be entered on punch cards and coordinates describing types and wares assembled in little piles of cardboards. This is pottery analysis, but it is not quite pottery acumen. The only computer that can understand the totality of ceramics is the human mind.

Index

(Note: Page numbers in italics refer to illustrations.)